THE ROAD TO ME II:
Dumping the Trash
GARY W. RICHMAN, PH.D.

ACKNOWLEDGEMENTS

I would first off like to acknowledge the Universe for its help and guidance. There are many high school counselors who would be shocked to learn that this dyslexic, reading disordered, less than mediocre student has written another book let alone one.

The next thanks must go to my editor Gretchen Kvistad who not only helps with my grammar and word usage, but keeps the focus of the book consistent with my goals and tone. I am truly indebted to her for her skills and respectful collaboration. I could not have been more fortunate than when she came to help me.

I want to acknowledge Georgia Deaver for great art work for the cover of this book. I also appreciate her patience with me as I struggled to picture and describe what I wanted. Thank you.

We all would like our parents to honor us with their sense of pride in what we do. I would like to thank my mother for hers. One is never too old to hear such important things.

I would like to acknowledge the long term friends I have who have always honored me with their respect, honesty, and caring. You have all been so valuable and important when things have gone well and more importantly not so well.

I would like to acknowledge my wife, Lisa. Though we are the mirror to each other's growth, which can be trying, she stays the course. She supports and encourages my work as not only a priority, but as important. She is a light of energy and power that is unequaled in most circles, and lets me know even in the difficult times that I am loved.

TABLE OF CONTENTS

THE ROAD TO ME

This book will explore the ways in which you can regain your true self, heal the wounds from childhood and begin to reap the rewards of being a healthier and more empowered person. It builds on some ideas which were explored in my first book, *The Road to Me*, and so as an introduction to those of you who may not be familiar with these ideas, I will briefly touch on them here. If you have already read and are familiar with these ideas, please feel free to skip to the Introduction.

As good as you are, as great as you are and as complete as you are, there is always more. That "more" lies in the unconscious psychological DNA which depicts how we see ourselves at this core DNA level and how the world sees us. And once that is cemented, it drives our behavior until we unlearn it. The continued behavior patterns that manifest from this behavior is what I call the "learned personality."

We develop our learned personality through our experiences in our childhood. This learned personality is made up of all of our psychological baggage, which I will call "trash" from our childhood, and is cemented into our psyche at a core level by the age of ten. This personality is what I refer to as the learned personality, likened to the psychological DNA, and this personality feels permanent and immutable to us. The bad news is that these feelings can bring about self-sabotage, helplessness and despair of ever having a whole and healthy life. The good news is that this personality IS NOT immutable; and as it was once learned, it can be unlearned at the same psychological DNA level.

This learned personality is indoctrinated by our primary caregivers and as we breathed in the air of this environment they created, we are constantly adjusting and accommodating to this reality. Too many people stay away from doing their psychological work because they feel it's all about blaming their parents. Dismantling the personality that was created in this environment is the first step toward healing. Because we breathed in this (sometimes toxic) air, or drank the Kool-Aid, as it were, our first step needs to be giving our parents the responsibility for creating the air, and offering us the Kool-Aid.

We believe, as small children, that our parents are divine. That life revolves around us and our needs and that all will be well if we can just get our parent to listen to us when we ask for something we need. In a perfect world this would work, and we would have a whole society of walking, talking, divine, aware people on this earth. The reality, however, is that while we as children are trying to believe that all will be well, and that the divine (dare I say omnipotent) people that we call parents will always be there for us, is just not true.

The problem is that our parents are only human. They too have been raised in a family with its foibles, problems and sometimes severely damaging patterns. They themselves are struggling to be whole, healthy and aware people and they may simply not have the skills or abilities to be a good parent. They may be distant, emotionally detached, narcissistic or even addicts of one sort or another.

All of these things make up the flawed people that <u>should</u> be there for the child, but often aren't. And in order to make these divine parents happy, the child often learns to subjugate, suppress and stifle their wants, needs & desires; often at the expense of their power or spirit. We are born with our power, then willingly give it up through submission to our parents in exchange for the hope of being cherished and loved.

Many people cannot imagine themselves as any different or any more than they already are. They believe that who they have known themselves to be is all they can be. If, for example, you have always known yourself to be passive, unlucky, or not loveable, you may then believe you will always be these things. Based on your past, what else could you believe? How could your personal reality be any different?

To feel empowered is the very foundation of confidence, compassion, strength, and mastery. It is the ability to be all you can be without giving up any part of yourself, and without inviting attack or ridicule even though you are open and vulnerable. Many people cannot imagine a way to be vulnerable and also to be safe. But when you know who you are, combining the strength of your intellect with open and genuine feelings enables you to share your true self completely and to remain totally safe.

The Road to Me: Reclaiming Your Power puts into plain language a way of understanding psychotherapy as a method of undoing the "learned" sense of self in order to embrace our own true self. It is a means to help you "get out of your own way" so that you can reclaim and actualize your personal power. It offers a clear path for helping individuals to heal and to become better acquainted with themselves. It is a precursor to embracing one's soul. To become aware of the soul is to touch those parts of our selves that house the higher self – the essence within.

INTRODUCTION

Consider this a textbook which can help you recognize the repetitive, negative patterns that can trash and sabotage your life and give you the tools to begin to change those patterns. Not only that, this book can show you how to walk this earth so confident in your true self that you will be able to defend yourself from verbal attack, sure in the knowledge that you are a true child of light and immune to the petty put-downs and mean sarcasm of others. You also won't find it necessary to verbally attack or belittle others, and will be able to get your emotional needs met on a fundamental level by communicating honestly and fearlessly to the ones that you love.

Sound like psychobabble nonsense to you? Okay, well let's take these ideas one by one and see where we go. We all develop our learned personality in our childhood. This learned personality is populated with all our psychological baggage, which I will call "trash" from our wounded childhood. This trash is a culmination of our subconscious miss-beliefs that sabotage our walk through life. We are taught these miss-beliefs by our immediate caretakers during childhood, and they may have included some of the following:

- ☐ I'm not lovable
- ☐ I'm not worthy
- ☐ I'm undeserving
- ☐ I'm not heard
- ☐ I don't deserve to be happy
- ☐ I'm not desirable
- ☐ I'm not cherished

- ☐ I'm not bright/smart

- ☐ I'm not capable

- ☐ I'm not trustworthy
- ☐ I'm invisible
- ☐ I'm not listened to
- ☐ I'm not worth nurturing
- ☐ I'm not worth staying with
- ☐ I'm not appreciated
- ☐ I'm not worthy of attention
- ☐ I'm not worth protecting
- ☐ I can't be successful

Now read that list again and mentally put a checkmark in the box next to the miss-beliefs that resonate with you. This resonance lets you know where you hold negative beliefs about your self which were taught to you by your parents and which were cemented at a core level by the time you turned ten years old. At this time, our belief changes from knowing that we are a true, divine child of the Universe/God to someone whose ego is second-guessing themselves. This process virtually replaces the essence of our inner divinity with a nagging sense of loathing, self-doubt, insecurity and fear, which is housed in what I refer to as our "learned psychological DNA."

Here's the truth - what you can learn in this book is that (are you ready for this?).......NONE OF THESE THINGS ARE TRUE. None of the foregoing statements represent who you are – these were things that you were *taught, and so, like a bad habit, can be unlearned and replaced with healthy, positive messages.*

This book, as much as I would like it to be, is not a quick fix. It will not solve all your problems and make you healthier, happier, and living in your truth for the first time in your life. It will, however, help you identify those areas which are holding you back from realizing your true potential. Knowing this, you are armed with the most powerful information I can give you: what you need to work on to be the child of the Universe/God that you once were.

So, what are the ramifications of forgetting our connection to the Universe/God from childhood until sometime in our adult life when we decide to do our work and reclaim our inner child? Well, for one, it <u>does</u> mean that we have walked life with an emptiness inside that manifests in personal sabotage, feeling alone, possibly depressed and separated from our core and the Universe. It <u>does</u> <u>not</u> mean however, that our connection to our divinity has died. It <u>does</u> mean that as a child of the Universe/God, our connection, which is always there for the asking, has been smothered by the trash of our learned personality.

Next, the tools to change. By understanding our miss-beliefs, we can begin to heal them. We begin to understand that the whole purpose for being here is to walk as a child of light, which we are impeded from doing. *We* create our own roadblocks to success and happiness by not recognizing negative, repetitive patterns which do not serve us. We also ignore the so-called "coincidences" which occur in our day to day lives which give us the opportunity to change, if only we acted on them. There are no such things as coincidences; only messages sent from the universe which we can choose to act on, or not.

You need to stop thinking that it is all just coincidence and realize that the Universe is tapping you on the shoulder for a reason and, **it ain't going away**. And what is really important to know is that, if you <u>refuse</u> to pay attention to these repetitive patterns in your life, the Universe will keep upping the ante by hitting you with <u>a bigger stick</u>/life example until you pay attention. So when you hear yourself say, why can't I ever learn? That is exactly the question you should be asking yourself, only re-frame "can't" to "won't."

One of the ways we can make sense of these difficult ideas is to think about these connections. We are all connected in the unified field of oneness; that is, we are all humans, made up of the same stuff and living our lives together. Our shared human experiences make us connected – we all laugh, cry and love, are born and die. And we all, ALL of us, have been taught miss-beliefs by those of us who were meant to be caretakers. Once we heal the wounds of our ego and shed our learned subconscious miss-beliefs, we can begin living (again) as a true child of light, and will be able to see others with the same compassion, love and respect that we hold for our selves.

Ah, one more thing about this book you should probably know: this is not a novel; or a book to be read cover to cover. Take your time, read some, put it down, ruminate, come back and read some more. It isn't meant to be taken in one big gulp. Hopefully it will make you realize some really hard, possibly uncomfortable things which will require some processing time. These are important lessons for all of us to recognize, and I hope you find value in them.

SECTION I

SUBCONSCIOUS (NEGATIVE) MISS-BELIEFS

The core of your divine self is always there, under all the accumulated "trash" from your childhood. The key is to shed the trash, unearth the true, pure you and be able to accept that this is your new reality – the new "it."

What does this all mean? It means that we will be focusing on how sabotage due to miss-beliefs show up in your life subconsciously through repetitive behaviors that cause you to be in your way and unhealthy. These miss-beliefs are taken in on a core, psychological DNA level based on experiences taken in during birth through age ten as they are taken in from the gods of your universe i.e., parents. These repetitive behaviors are debilitating over time as they cause you to be constantly in your way.

It is my professional belief that you must engage a competent psychotherapist to work through this process. Many people do not understand the courage it takes to go after this arduous and scary work. This book will give you a way to identify the warning signs that these patterns are beginning to show up and the tools to diffuse them. This section will focus on the various ways that these behaviors manifest, giving you a map on how to identify, unlearn and correct them.

CHAPTER 1

SOULS HAVING A HUMAN EXPERIENCE

So what does "souls having a human experience" mean in the context of living life and dumping subconscious trash? Well, everything. I propose that we are souls housed in the containers called bodies to walk on "playground earth" to learn our lessons. We are the God energy; the Universal connection to the One, a soul witnessing and watching from the gallery of life, examining the data. It is from this data that we learn more about our selves, while not getting caught up or fighting what we see. It is not acting out insecure issues of our miss-beliefs, but looking at what the data means in terms of our own shortcomings to become whole.

My friend and radio co-host Dr. Bill Little, Ph.D., physicist and minister, told me a story about this. He said that the whole of who we are is a duality; like two birds in a tree. One bird will fly down to the ground to find food and get caught up with other birds in the petty exchanges of life. The second bird sits high up in the tree witnessing the events of life and evaluates the situation. This is like our inner witness and our ego. The inner witness is here to do just that; it can't be seen or tangibly detected, but it is taking in the data of our daily encounters providing lessons that we choose we can decipher and learn from, hence becoming more conscious. Like Shakespeare's idea that "All the world's a stage and we are just players on it" (*As you Like It,* II. vii. 139-143), I contend that the stage is akin to the bird on the ground. It is here that we play out are roles based on learned subconscious miss-beliefs that are like scripts.

Eric Berne, in his book *Games People Play,* talks about the scripts of life we are all caught up in. This is our ego acting in the world amidst those we are here to interact with. These interactions offer us experiences that are data configured to give us the lessons we are here in this lifetime to learn. As this data is being downloaded, the witness can work at dismantling the ego's "data," which is in the way of manifesting one's true self. Therefore, if you invest in this mindset, and not the typical Western orientation of rationalization and denial, then some important work can be accomplished.

So as the data from the play of daily life is downloaded, the witness can then take a look at what the film industry calls the "dailies." We can analyze, learn and unlearn from the experience. As one becomes more conscious and aware, the fine-tuning of the witness is accomplished as the individual gets a healthy distance from the "stage." The great thing about this is that out of this fine-tuning comes an evolved self or detached awareness that does not take the play personally, but is all about the observations. This perspective is imperative from this juncture that there is less psychological wounding available to trigger the personality, which previously caused inappropriate or tantrum like behavior. Therefore, you are completely free to attend to the input, process the information, and expand and contribute to your higher purpose. What I call dumping the subconscious trash of the miss-beliefs, to reclaim your true self.

The self, which I liken to the ego, i.e., the 'learned personality" has its wounds of insecurity, inadequacy, neediness, and fears of abandonment, which pollute your ability to be an efficient collector of "the data." This is the first bird. It is polluted because the perspective from which we are ascertaining this data and evaluating it is flawed. It is flawed because the "learned personality" described in my first book, *The Road To Me: Reclaiming Your Power* is built on subconscious learned miss-beliefs[1] of self, which is not our true or core nature. It is the false input from our flawed primary caregivers' system, which has without malice or deliberateness inputted data into our psychological DNA, facilitating a lesser, more damaged belief of self.

Therefore, as we are collecting data from this wounded perspective, we act on false beliefs of self, projections, and assumptions based on childhood. In essence, what we have come to hold as the reality of who we are is based on learned miss-beliefs. We believe this reality to be our true sense of self, and run our daily life through this biased software or screen, which can be likened to one's hard drive.

---

1 I repeat this term many times to keep implanting the notion of how powerful the miss-beliefs are in negatively impacting your life.

We live in a reality based on childhood cellular mapping, which seems as real to us as if we had goggles on and were watching some type of virtual reality.

In fact, this is a good analogy. Our perspective of our selves is virtual, and not our core self. We know this to be so because as we continue to change, our inner mapping of held onto miss-beliefs still plagues and sabotages us. It is this mapping that we are here to eradicate. Hence, we don't even have an awareness that the second bird, the witness, exists. By working on consciousness and healing our wounded subconscious miss-beliefs, we begin to walk toward re-claiming the witness.

The following exemplifies this where a client of mine could not imagine that he was holding a miss-belief of self that keep getting in his way. He could not see any other way of handling repetitive situations as they came up:

CLIENT: *I have come to you because I keep getting into fights at bars even though I am not looking for trouble.*

DR. R.: *What seems to happen as you walk into the bars?*

CLIENT: *Well it could be any night. I go in, minding my own business and for no apparent reason some guy will walk up to me and get in my face.*

DR. R.: *As best you can recreate tell me how you go into the bar, and what happens as you are there.*

CLIENT: *Well, I walk in and look around and then go to the bar and order a drink. I say hello to those I know and then I just hang out.*

DR. R.: *Ok, now as you are hanging out tell me anything that stands out in the crowd.*

CLIENT: *I'm not sure. I just look around and see who's there, however, I do notice when there is someone who seems to be looking for trouble.*

DR. R.: *What do you mean?*

CLIENT: *There is almost always someone who is looking to get into it with someone. You know, the guy with the extra grudge or testosterone issue.*

DR. R.: *What do you do when you see him?*

CLIENT: *Well, I am just not the kind of guy who looks away when someone is eye- balling me.*

DR. R.: *You mean that when someone is trolling for a fight or staring, you don't blink.*

CLIENT: *Well, yea. I am not going to let someone think they can get over on me.*

DR. R.: *So if they are looking for trouble and eyeball you, you hold their gaze.*

CLIENT: *Yea.*

DR. R.: *Ok, so if they are looking for the person who is going to meet their need to fight, you accommodate.*

CLIENT: *I never quite looked at it that way.*

DR. R.: *You need to see that they need to get into conflict for their own reasons, and when you accommodate them, they win.*

CLIENT: *I hold my own pretty well, they don't always win.*

DR. R.: *What I mean is that if they need to fight and you accommodate, they get their needs met, even if they lose the fight.*

CLIENT: *Oh, I see what you mean.*

DR. R.: *Where did you learn the miss-belief that you have to hold your own or they win?*

CLIENT: *From my dad. He was one son of a bitch mean guy. He would rage and sometimes smack me around.*

DR. R.: *So since he abused you, you won't let that happen again.*

CLIENT: *Yea. I swore that when I got big enough, no one was ever again going to push me around or be in my face and get away with it.*

DR. R.: *So you can see that the miss-belief you have is that you have to take on anyone who postures in your direction even if they have no idea who you are.*

CLIENT: *What do you mean?*

DR. R.: *I mean that these guys in the bars aren't there for you; they are there for anyone who will oblige them in an altercation. It is they who need to fight and your old buttons react when you see these guys.*

CLIENT: *Oh, I see what you mean. I give them a target to go after because of what my dad did to me.*

DR. R.: *Yes and in doing so, no matter who wins the fight, they win because they got what they came for.*

A second example is:

CLIENT: *I grew up in a religion and in a family that told me that I was not right and never did things appropriately. I am married to a guy who treats me with disrespect and is verbally mean to me.*

DR. R.: *What did you hear from your family and community?*

CLIENT: *My dad always told me that I was not smart and that I had better marry someone who could take care of me. The religion I grew up in told me that the world was a place of sin, and that only our community knew how to live and be loved by God.*

DR. R.: *How did that feel as you grew up?*

CLIENT: *It felt like crap. I couldn't belong with my friends at school and I never felt right with the beliefs of my church.*

DR. R.: *So no matter where you were, you were not good enough and felt like an outsider whomever you were with.*

CLIENT: *Yes that is exactly how I felt.*

DR. R.: *And how does that fit in with your marriage?*

CLIENT: *When I first met my husband he seemed like a great guy, but over some years after we were married he got really angry at how I did things and what decisions I would make.*

DR. R.: *How would he show that rage over time?*

CLIENT: *He would say awful things about me and at times hit me.*

DR. R.: *What caused you to stay after he stepped over the line and abused you?*

CLIENT: *I kept thinking if only I could do it right he would see that I had a good heart and was worth loving.*

DR. R.: *How did that work?*

CLIENT: *It didn't. He only got worse and more out of hand.*

DR. R.: *It sounds like you grew up with the miss-belief that you were inadequate and everyone from your dad to God told you if you could just get it "right," you would be deserving of love.*

CLIENT: *[begins to cry] That is exactly what I have believed.*

DR. R.: *In the subconscious you have been looking to continually prove yourself to the point of finding a husband who won't see your goodness. It's like you are trying to get a blind man to see you, believing his damage must be due to your shortcoming.*

CLIENT: *Yes, it is what I believe.*

DR. R.: *These are the miss-beliefs we all hold to some degree from our dysfunctional childhoods that need to be worked on and healed.*

In these examples, we see how we are stuck in the ego's miss-beliefs, which leaves us vulnerable to anyone's scrutiny. You react from the implanted psychological DNA of the subconscious, not from your better/higher self. You are like the bird on the ground, i.e., caught up in the mess without any healthy, higher perspective. Only when you get in touch with your miss-beliefs and dismantle them, hence unlearn the subconscious teachings, can you begin to have the perspective and growth offered by the bird in the tree.

I can imagine how this is pushing the envelope. It is certainly out there for many, depending on how familiar you are with these concepts. So let's back up a bit. It is the belief system of many that we are here in this lifetime, as stated earlier, to learn our lessons. Even if you don't hold this belief, is it fair to say from your belief system that growing and learning from life experiences can help you to be a better person and result in accomplishing more? This is pretty basic to all who have lived more than a couple of decades.

So whatever the growth system you ascribe to, can you agree that self-evolution can be considered a worthwhile thing? If you can agree with this concept, then there must be a component of self that is out there engaging and experiencing the lessons, while another part of you is taking in the research and synthesizing the data. It is obvious that there must be a part of you that is experiencing some input on the experiential plane, hence what I have referred to as the bird on the ground or the one caught up in the play.

In essence, you are too close to the action and therefore cannot be detached, or gain the unemotional perspective needed to look at the experience. Therefore, for growth and perspective to occur another part of you must be available to analyze the data from the experience, or as the metaphor goes, be the bird in the tree or the witness in the audience. This bird in the tree or the witness is taking detached and unemotional notation, processing and analyzing what is occurring for the bigger picture, which focuses on personal, conscious evolution. Thus looking at life's purpose, which facilitates, as Buddha would say, "being awake."

As I outlined in my first book, the subconscious need overrides the conscious want until you unlearn and heal learned miss-beliefs which caused you to get in your way. As the witness becomes the focus around your experiences, you get deeper insights as to why you repeatedly act out certain patterned behaviors that sabotage your life. The more you realize how these subconscious learned miss-beliefs play out in your life, the more you heal these wounds and begin to come from a keener "aware" state of mind and self. Therefore, through healing these subconscious learned miss-beliefs, they have less power to control your life.

From this vantage point, you strengthen the witness while becoming a more empowered individual. As this occurs you take on better, healthier scripts and the actor/ego on stage gets to be involved in plays that bring peace, joy, abundance, and contentment to the self. Hence, you begin to reclaim your true self while reality and life as you know it shifts for the better. Thus, the ego gets a job upgrade because the data coming in is processed in a healthier manner, and one's whole being begins to relax more into a life. Your roles in the plays get more satisfying and productive, if not actually joyous and abundant.

This relaxation around life takes on another wonderful perspective because as you step away more from the insecurities that have been running your behavior, you do not take anything too personally. As you are more empowered, you are less subject to people's petty accusations and slurs. Your perspective is more in the audience than on the stage. From this vantage point, though you are saddened by how the other actors reduce themselves to immature interactions; the good news is that you are not one of them. This is the "aware" part of consciousness with regard to what is going on around you, while not being caught up in it. Hence you are witnessing the events of the play, but are not a part of the drama, i.e., caught up in the reactive triggering that causes personal harm, but able to sit in a healthy and detached perspective.

Until we remember that our true inner state of being is an empowered divine self, we will continue to struggle along without unlearning the ego. The lessons of life experiences will occur and keep reoccurring for the benefit of the individual to "get it." The "getting it" is described above and it is always amazing to see how consistent we are at subconsciously bringing in the right examples to learn from. Hence the biblical quote of, "…it will be done for you just as you have believed" (Matthew 8:13). Many know this biblical text, but how closely do we look at what it means or how it plays out in our lives? If everything is a part of the "one" as quantum physics and Eastern philosophies espouse; and if movies like *What the #$*! do we (k)now!?* and *Secrets* are correct on particle theory and/or laws of attraction, then do we create our own reality and attract it to our stage?

In 1979 Robin Williams recorded his first comedy album, and named it *Reality...What a concept!* I tell the people I work with that reality is a solid, stable force. However, I also believe that the ultimate, true reality is not where most of us hang out or live. I believe it is a continuum from 1 to 100 where 100 is the true living space of reality. I therefore believe that most of us live somewhere in between one and one hundred with our reality of the world and our selves changing every decade or so. If you think about it most of us who have lived awhile are not in the same mind set/reality as we were in our teens, twenties, or thirties. As this is so, our reality which we thought of as our selves and our world is not the same and always changing.

Taking the above as so, you can see how this can impact and affect our daily lives. How you say? Well if we know that our concept of reality is just that, a concept, then wherever we are is just a stepping stone to the next level toward "reality." If we hold this to be true than we are never at the end, but just in process. If we are always in process then the sky is the limit as to what we can achieve in our lives. Too many people believe that who they are is **it** and where they are is **it**. Is it a concept and not the ultimate reality if we choose to be in process and intention more?

How then do we harness this on a practical daily basis? Most people want the Cliffs notes version which employs the quick fix method of hard work. Many do not want to put in the hard intellectual, emotional, and spiritual work involved in making their dreams come true. Would you expect to get into physical shape by just wanting it, reading a book, or watching a video? Of course not.

However, too many people want to achieve abundance and success by this magical thinking. It takes tangible effort and spiritual practices to manifest what you want. It is believing and follow through that makes things happen, not seeing is believing waiting it to show up. There was a movie quote in Steven Segal's movie *Under Siege 2,* which said 'luck favors the prepared mind.' It is when we go after something knowing that the reality of who we are and where we can go is not set in stone nor clear. The only limits we have are those miss-beliefs that were implanted/ brainwashed into our core psychological DNA as children.

Only as we get out of our own way and take our selves out for a test drive so to speak as to what we can truly achieve will we have our answer. Creating this whole and healthy human being comes out of the merging described above which is the results from consciousness. Consciousness is the new awareness and wisdom that comes from the hard work of uniting an unaccepted inner child with the soul seeking adult.

To move more into our inner truth and our God given right to empowerment, we must do the healing of the "inner child." This is where, Dr. Bill Little and I on our radio show of old, <u>Heart and Soul</u> would say, you must heal the wounds of the ego to move toward your highest good. In that we are souls having a human experience, we must go after the early, deep inner wounds that still project out in subtle and not so subtle behaviors of sabotage.

CHAPTER 2

THE REJECTED INNER CHILD

The next trashcan item needing to be dumped to get "there" is the miss-belief that our inner child is bad and unacceptable. This is the belief system wired in from childhood that says we are not acceptable. This learning occurred as we were unable to get the perfect loving from those beings who were looming around called mom and dad, who we thought were actually divine mother and father. From this miss-belief, we "try" to get the love we need and instinctively felt we deserve, but the more we "tried" the more our inner child felt unworthy.

Therefore, subconsciously we identify with those who do not like the child and push that inner child to the side. In doing so, we hoped that this would get the attention of the divine parents, i.e., getting them to bestow their altruistic love and adoration on us. This of course never happens because it is mom and dad that were our parents, who were not only lacking in the divine, they were dysfunctional. The goal of therapy is to recognize this, let go of the myth, and stop holding your life in abeyance waiting and hoping for divine mother and father to show up and bless you.

The glitch is that within this process of waiting, we keep pushing the inner child back into a dark place until not only are we out of touch with our true self, we have lost all recollection of being divine. In fact, we end up feeling unacceptable to whatever degree of dysfunction we own. On top of that, the inner child has been living without nurturance, trust, security, protection, acceptance, love, comfort, closeness, and dare I say, Light.

This inner being does not hold a sense that anyone could care enough to love him/her, nor that he/she could possibly be worth anyone's time. (Of course there are degrees of this, which are determined by the first eight years of life and the level of dysfunction within the family system. If the family system was healthier so too will be the inner child. Therefore, to the degree that the family system was seriously dysfunctional, so too will the inner child be and your own subconscious disdain of it).

So you can see where this is leading. First, if your inner child has even a moderate degree of self-loathing as described above, he/she may consciously want to have a healthy, loving, well supported, successful life. However, if the subconscious holds a personal lack of acceptance and worth, then only a limited amount of positive feeling can be allowed to surface. This is due to the subconscious underpinnings that consistently tell you that you are undeserving, which are supporting you.

I say to my clients that the subconscious need will always override the conscious want. This shows up in subtle and not so subtle patterns of sabotage. An example would be someone whose subconscious holds a sense that he/she doesn't deserve to be loved unconditionally; hence they would draw toward themselves someone who can only love conditionally. And they would repeat this pattern until the inner child is convinced he or she is worthy of Love.

Often clients will talk about meeting someone who is healthy, fun, smart, sane, and loving. However, after a while they report that the relationship ended because they just got bored with the person or did not feel the "juice" necessary to promote the relationship. This may happen in the early throws of the courtship or even a year down the road, but the reason is often the same: boredom. Here again, they found what it is that they consciously want, i.e., an accepting, loving person that they don't have to prove anything to. But it is not acceptable to the subconscious.

Of course, you know what happens next; they find someone who completely turns them on and stimulates all the right buttons, has all the right juice, and they are sure they are in love as this is "the one." Then about six months to two years later they are miserable because this love of their life has various familiar features of being cold, distant, difficult to care for, demeaning, and unavailable. They are in agony over the fact that once again they are feeling as if they are not enough, and have to (unsuccessfully) prove themselves to this partner. They are torn up and devastated that something that started out so right and was seemingly nothing like the bad relationships from their past once again ended up in the same hurtful, heartbreaking place. Again the subconscious need (the psychological DNA is a miss-belief that they are unlovable, undeserving, and unworthy) overrides the conscious want for a healthy, accepting, loving relationship.

The task is to re-raise the little one to realize that he/she is not any of those learned subconscious miss-beliefs that are held as the reality of self. That our little one, though wounded and suffering from the emotional abandonment from parents and our selves, is a wonderful child of the Universe and deserving of everything.

The first step is to begin the work of psychotherapy where you learned at that psychological DNA level that you were not deserving or lovable and what you still own of that. This is what I call unlearning the learned personality. It is the deeper work that is necessary to kick out the miss-beliefs that are defining you. This is done for whatever time it takes for the inner child to reveal him/herself to me. [Now this is dicey because you were right with me until I brought up what seems like some psychobabble nonsense, which seems to make no sense].

It is an intangible that at some time in therapy the inner child makes itself known to me in a way where I almost say hello to it. If this were a movie, I would orchestrate it by having a therapy session where a little child's head sticks out through the chest of the client and says, "Hi." It is almost that literal for me and it never fails to happen. I recognize the child, say "Hi" back and own that the real work is now on the table. As this is real to me I begin to tailor the work around the heart with the client getting him/her to begin owning feelings and perspectives from that area. As we do this and the client feels more comfortable at this level of exchange, I move to the next step.

This next step, which shows up at some point down the road of the therapy, is where I have the client engage the little one in an exercise that is designed to help reunite one's adult with the inner child. This is done for two reasons: 1) to reintroduce contact and an offering of acceptance and protection from your adult to the child, which the child no longer has any sense of deserving; and 2) to reengage the child with the adult reclaiming the joy, playfulness, creativity, intuition and wonderment that is the child.

This exercise is simple but profound and will often bring up a number of emotions and memories that need careful and patient processing. It starts by imagining that you are in a hallway with no lights. You sit down cross-legged on the floor and light a candle. *(You are visualizing yourself sitting on the floor because your inner child will be represented at the age that they were relegated to the dark [usually around 5-10]; and even sitting on a chair or standing in the hallway would not make them feel safe. The candle represents a small amount of light and exposure, which will not overwhelm the child.)*

As you sit on the floor in the visualization gently invite the child out. (I often tell clients that the child is probably behind a door or in another room off the hallway and is anxious to come out.) Therefore, you want to make this an invitation that offers control to the inner child and in no way feels like a demand or a threat. The child will poke its head out for you can imagine its loneliness and pain. It will be reticent as there is no reason to really trust you. Remember, you subconsciously put that child in the dark as a means to gain acceptance and love from your parents or primary caregivers. (This is a survival mechanism, for when we are given consistent messages that we are unacceptable we make an unconscious choice to abandon that part of self that we perceive to be in the way of our gaining acceptance).

Hence, trust has to be regained as only trust can; with patience and time. So, as you sit in your visualization you gently coax your inner child to approach. Now what I say to clients is to really look at the child that shows up in your visualization. They may look scared, anxious, small, shy, lean, angry, hurt, reticent, or disbelieving. All of this is expected and normal. It is the job of the adult to be completely accepting of this child and his/her demeanor. As the child approaches, however close they come is also all right. You should have no expectations on how close your child will get. You accept and reinforce that whatever feels safe to them is fine.

I then ask the client to tell the little one honestly and exactly why all of this has occurred. The client starts by saying, with my help, that due to the system that we (both aspects of self- the adult and child) grew up in, I could not accept aspects of you that I was told were not acceptable. Thus, I pushed you aside and contributed to your rejection. I see now that this was wrong and you were just being a child who may have made mistakes or acted out as children do, but was not bad and had a right to be loved and cherished. I see how this hurt both of us and I want to make amends (you do all of this without an attachment to the outcome. It is just about coming from your truth and being heard from a genuine place).

I ask the client to continue with this exercise honestly expressing how all of this must have made the child feel. You, again with my help, as this is new and is difficult due to the nature of the wounds and their origins), tells the inner child that he/she must have felt deserted, abandoned, horribly alone, bad, unacceptable, unworthy, and less than. You let your inner child know that you understand that any child would be mistrusting of someone venturing forth all of a sudden, and be suspect of any warmth or love. You let your inner child know that you get that this is so, and you are not asking the child to trust or believe you at this moment. However, you let the inner child know that you are coming from true intention, and that you are going to keep saying it until the child takes it in as truth.

This exercise is repeated daily or certainly weekly until you experience the child move closer towards you with trust. The goal is to have the child come and sit in your lap and eventually go out for walks and play with you. As this continues, it need <u>not</u> be attached to a timetable. This could take ten minutes or ten months. It is the trust, while speaking your truth to your own inner self, that is essential. It is the reuniting, reconnecting, and rebuilding of trust that is the work.

Often, as the client does this work as I mentioned, many feelings and memories will surface. Feelings of being unacceptable and abandoned will show up. The memories will leave distaste in the client's mouth, and possible tears in his/her eyes. It is essential to talk about all of this as we proceed with the exercise so that understanding, emoting, and closure can occur.

The obvious result down the road is to reunite the adult with the child. By doing this, the unity and wholeness of the two accepting each other again and reconnecting brings a peace and strength to the individual. It also propagates the reuniting of the protective, strength, and unconditional loving aspect of the adult with the creative, imagination, passion, and joy of the child. Hence, there exists a whole and healthy being.

CHAPTER 3

CONSCIOUSNESS

The idea of consciousness has been bantered around so much, it is hard to even imagine what else could possibly be said about this. However, stay with me as I just might add some flavor to this already well-known entity.

How can we get "there," dump the trash, eradicate learned subconscious miss-beliefs, make changes, or become personally empowered if we are unaware of what is going on around us or inside of us? The Buddha was asked who he was; he was also asked to respond to many questions about himself and his answer was silence. People pleaded with him to answer the baffling question of who he was; finally, he gave in and his answer was simple: "I am awake," he said.

We could take the obvious understandings as to what consciousness is and say that those who have their eyes closed and are sleeping are unconscious, while those who have their eyes open are conscious. We could also say that those who are in a coma are not awake, and those watching over the patient are awake. As John Muir said, "most people are on the world, not in it - having no conscious sympathy or relationship to anything about them – undiffused, separate, and rigidly alone like marbles of polished stone, touching but separate."

It is not having our senses operational which defines being conscious or awake. It is our deep inner processing from a non-judgmental position that takes in information for the sole purpose of expanding our own relationship to our self. Therefore, there are degrees of awake and there is being fully awake. There are degrees of consciousness and there is being fully conscious. It is the journey of taking out our inner, learned trash and getting completely real with ourselves and stepping out of our known self into the witness perspective that unites us with the Universe.

So, what the heck does that mean? Well, let's take that and expand it to every aspect of life that is you. If we live in the subconscious state of fog then we fumble from pillar to post without growth or change. Many people, and there are many who choose to live in this state of denial and rationalization, are always amazed when bad things keep "happening" to them over and over and over again.

It is like the movie *Groundhog Day*. In the story, the main protagonist keeps waking up each morning to repeat the same day he had the day before. He is stuck in time and is completely at a loss on how to free himself. At first he is just in shock, then he gets depressed, then he attempts suicide on a daily basis only to wake up the next morning in the same bed as the day before; repeating the same day. Finally, as he surrenders to his circumstances, things begin to shift as he becomes cognizant of what is going on around him, how it impacts him, his feelings, and how he impacts people's lives. And through his heightened state of consciousness, he learns compassion, humility and what love is. As he deepens into true consciousness he is released from his purgatory and wakes up to a brand new day of life, love, and reality.

Throughout most of this movie, the male protagonist is unconscious; only thinking of his own needs and what he can get from others. If you stay in such a narcissistic orientation, your life is virtual hell punctuated by disappointment and loneliness. What is the saying that so many victims say: "same story different day" or "why does this keep happening to me?" It keeps happening because if you don't want to see, then you will remain stuck and blind. Most people keep their heads buried in the sand, playing ostrich, and have no relationship to their actions. They don't want to have to do the hard but glorious work of being mindful.

Most people live their lives based on the definition of insanity: doing the same thing over and over again expecting different results. They keep banging their heads against the same wall hoping it will become a door. And when the door doesn't appear, let alone open, they eat more, drink more, do more drugs, have affairs, complain, recreate drama, project, distract, shame and blame. They will engage in <u>anything</u> but owning the responsibility for their actions...

...Anything but tweaking their perspective to come up with a different way of doing things.

…Anything but having to go to someone and say "I don't know how to do it."

…Anything but having to listen and take guidance from someone who knows.

…Anything but having to own the reality that they have lessons to learn and there is no way around that.

Most westerners don't like to admit they are wrong or that they don't know something, or to apologize. They are not in a healthy relationship with themselves; assessing their inner motivators or repetitive patterns that are defining and running them. A friend of mine, Dr. Rick Moss says, "If you want to know what you want, look at what you have." There was a quote in a movie (I love referencing movies that offer poignant reminders) that stated the choices you make dictate the life you lead. Another movie references this with the idea that everything you do is a choice and there are no victims...

So many people don't want to look, while others only want to blame. We would rather be in a relationship with others projecting out and finding fault with anyone other than our selves. We badly don't want to see the repetitive subconscious patterns stemming from our miss-beliefs, hence the guideposts indicating the extent to which we are in our way. There's a common myth perpetuated in the west that the Chinese symbol for crises is opportunity, and most successful people will tell you that it was their personal failures that brought them to their triumphs. They had the courage, insight, and demeanor to look and keep learning.

To be unconscious is to sit in the narrow clutches of being constricted, alone, and unsuccessful. We are caught in a world where we feel out of control and unable to negotiate our way. We feel that we are at the mercy of happenstance and coincidence. That is no way to know what is our next step and that all we can do in the extreme is to accept our fate, suffer and die.

As we step into consciousness we expand, risk, invite the Universe to play on our team, which by the way brings what is referred to as luck. Luck comes to those who have the courage to risk and reach. As we reach out, we go beyond ourselves, expanding to new heights. This expansion lends itself to being tuned in and consciously observing where we are going, what is happening, and how we got there. This is the essence of being in relationship with self, thus taking ownership of what is going on inside of us, and being on purpose. An example of this occurred with a client of mine in therapy:

CLIENT: *I love my wife, but every time that I want her to do something for me she acts like I am giving her an order or pushing her around.*

DR. R.: *Do you ask her why she feels that way?*

CLIENT: *I did ask her and she said that I don't ever step up and give freely to her and she resents it.*

DR. R.: *Women, according to John Grey's Men Are from Mars, Women Are from Venus, use 'always' and 'never' when they mean that it occurs most of the time. Men get caught up in words rather than working on what might be contributing to the problem. It may be that your wife does not feel that you are as invested in offering support as you are of requesting it of her.*

CLIENT: *I have no idea what that means. I am always doing something around the house or taking the kids somewhere. All I am asking is for her to show me that she sees my efforts.*

DR. R.: *Did you ever think that she might be in need of the same thing?*

CLIENT: *I only want some acknowledgement that she sees how hard I work.*

DR. R.: *From that perspective is it possible that you are harsh when you request her to get something for you because you are really demanding that she sees how hard you work?*

CLIENT: *I suppose that might be fueling my responses. I hadn't thought of it that way.*

DR. R.: *Most people are unconscious to the motivators that are "fueling" their responses. If you are feeling unappreciated, it would go a long way if you were to tell her that instead of making her prove something. Men are not good with expressing their* *feelings. They go to control and demands when they could be really saying they feel alone, unappreciated or even missing the company or nurturing of their wives.*

CLIENT: *But if I say that to her she will think I am a wuss.*

DR. R.: *You know you are not alone in that feeling. I work with a lot of men who like us were brought up that tough and guarded are the only way to be. And in this world, where the mentality of competition rules the boardrooms, they are not wrong. But we hopefully choose our woman based on their warmth and compassion. When we relate from that heart space with our woman, they feel connected to us and needed; none of which is a bad thing. The tough part is that we have to do something that goes completely against our grain: be vulnerable.*

CLIENT: *That certainly is a different way of looking at it. So if I tell my wife that I need more appreciation and acknowledgement, I might not have the edge in my voice when I ask her to do something. Maybe I won't ask her for as much if I felt her consistently supporting me.*

DR. R.: *Right. Being honest means being vulnerable and that's hard, but the rewards are worth it.*

It is ever so important that we work on consciousness to understand what makes us tick, and even more importantly, what causes us to be triggered and act out inappropriately. When we do not take stock of how we feel or what our deeper feelings[2] are, they get permission to act out from our egoistic states of insecurities, fears, and exclusion.

Another example of consciousness and the client:

CLIENT: *I don't know why I keep getting angry at family members.*

DR. R: *What seems to happen?*

CLIENT: *That's the trouble, I don't know. I just blow up at them for no apparent reason and I regret it.*

DR. R: *OK. It seems that there is something going on at a level that gets triggered and you act out the unconscious feelings. What seems to be happening when you are at a family gathering?*

CLIENT: *Well, I am listening to what somebody is saying and I feel myself getting frustrated and annoyed. Then I feel like I cannot hold on and I just want them to stop what they are saying.*

DR. R: *If I were there at that moment and froze everyone and said to you what is this person saying or doing that is getting to you, what would you say to me?*

---

2 What I mean by this is most people have feelings. As I say to those I work with, you do feel sadness, anger, and joy, but the level of the feelings I am talking about and where we work is at that deeper psychological DNA level. This deeper level is where even the most intelligent people I work with when asked what they feel typically answer, "I don't know."

CLIENT: *I would say that they were being like my family and I don't want to see it.*

DR. R: *In what way are they being like your family?*

CLIENT: *They are saying things that are like it was.*

DR. R: *Stay with that.*

CLIENT: *They are being victims and whining life when we grew up. It reminds me how hopeless everything was (he begins to put his hands in his head and cry).*

DR. R: *I know this is hard but that pain and those tears have been in there a long time and they need to come out.*

CLIENT: *I can't believe this is coming up.*

DR. R: *These feelings of how it was to be a child, helpless to change anything have been going on all your life. They are feelings that have been unconscious and acting out through anger any time they get triggered. As long as they were not conscious, you could not have options on how to deal with them. So you get angry at the person who is bringing up this hurt inside of you and wanting to shut them down so as not to experience them.*

CLIENT: *(his tears increase) Yes that is what is happening and I feel so ashamed for putting that on my family members. I want that to stop it.*

DR. R: *I understand. Now that you are more aware of what the trigger is you can have options on how to handle it and we will work on this.*

CLIENT: *Yea I don't want to go after people for my hurts.*

DR. R: *I know. As I have said before I have a formula on how this works. I call it UC squared: Unconscious to consciousness to change. Only when something comes out of the unconscious into consciousness can it have the possibility of change.*

CLIENT: *Yes I remember you saying that. Now I get it and want it to change.*

DR. R: *We can do that.*

When we drop into consciousness and our inner truth, then we are at the beginning of moving to that heightened state of awareness. This next step entails living in an exalted place of bliss. From this perspective, we have mitigated the trash and can look beyond the waste heap to be able to see all around us. Only in this way can we be clear as to who we are, what we want, and where we want to go. We are not at the whim of our emotions and negative self-image, which only keeps us chasing an outside illusion of well-being.

CHAPTER 4

OUTSIDE IN VERSUS INSIDE OUT

One of the biggest, if not the granddaddy, of all miss-beliefs is that our sense of value and worth originates from outside validation rather than from within. We are brainwashed in Western society that the way to get "there," to gain acceptance and recognition for being worthwhile, is to obtain it from external, "acceptable" sources. The tragedy is that everything we do and everything we are is validated through how our actions are judged or deemed to be credible. As if we would take a serious look at how things work, and conclude that our own sense of wholeness and well-being could come from outside of ourselves.

Imagine throwing a pebble into the water and believing that the rings would begin at the farthest parameter and work its way in. If someone were to predict that you would look at him or her as if they had rocks in their head. The only way that rings will appear in the water after throwing in a pebble is from the point of impact. The nucleus by definition is at the center/core of everything. So too is it with our being-ness.

CLIENT: *I don't know where to find myself.*

DR. R.: *What does that mean?*

CLIENT: *I seem to be running and doing for everyone else and feel like I'm getting further and further away from myself.*

DR. R.: *You feel you have to attend to everyone else's agenda and needs.*

CLIENT: *Yes, that's right. It feels like everyone needs something and it is my job to take care of them.*

DR. R.: *You put everyone ahead of you as if the only way to feel worthwhile or complete is to have everyone's approval.*

CLIENT: *Well, I am not sure I want to put it that way, but yes.*

DR. R.: *I am not attempting to be critical and I apologize if it came across that way. I am attending to the process where you believe everyone else has a right to have their needs met and if you were to take care of your own you would be selfish.*

CLIENT: *Yes, that is right. I was brought up to believe that if you took care of your own issues then you were selfish and bad.*

DR. R.: *I have worked with many who were brought up by narcissistic or demanding immature parents who insisted* *that their children attend to the parents' needs. From this perspective you are brought up to believe that it's all or nothing. Either you are selfish or selfless and there is no in between.*

CLIENT: *Exactly; I have always felt that either you are one or the other.*

DR. R.: *Yes, and if you can only be selfish or selfless, I would always choose being selfless. However, those are not the only choices. The middle ground is what I call "self-focused." This is where you attend to strengthening yourself to be strong and available to others. For instance, think about the wheel on a bicycle. If you only attend to the spokes and not the hub, what do you think will eventually happen?*

CLIENT: *I guess the wheel would stop and the hub would break.*

DR. R.: *Exactly. If you only attend to the spokes, which in life is family, friends, job, finances, and issues, the hub, which is you, will wear down and break. Which is kind of what you have been feeling, like you are eroding.*

CLIENT: *That is how I feel.*

DR. R.: *If you attend to your self you are doing that which will allow you to stay healthy and be able to attend to the spokes.*

CLIENT: *Wow, I would have seen that as selfish.*

DR. R.: *Yes. Let me ask you this. When you fly on a commercial plane, what do they say to do when the cabin pressure drops and the oxygen masks drop?*

CLIENT: *They tell you to put the mask on others before yourself.*

DR. R.: *Coming from the all or nothing/selfish or selfless perspective I know why you would say that, but you are wrong. They tell you to put your own mask on first and then on your family or children.*

CLIENT: *Oh yea, you're right.*

DR. R.: *They know that if you are not self-focused and don't put your mask on first; you will become oxygen deprived and unable to help anyone else. Only when you are breathing, hence self-focused and strong, can you be clear enough to think and react appropriately to assist others.*

CLIENT: *Oh my, that makes so much sense. I see how backwards I was working it and why I would feel so down.*

DR. R.: *Yes when you embrace the idea of "self-focused" and give up being the self-less martyr that you were brought up to believe in, you take back your power.*

CLIENT: *This is like night and day. It feels great.*

DR. R.: *Yes, it is very cool.*

To redirect our empowerment and health inward is the only true path. We must focus inwardly rather than outwardly if we are going to claim ourselves and be able to remain strong and accomplished.

To truly grasp the origins of this, we have to go back to basic psychology. As babies we are naturally narcissistic. This means that we believe that we are the center of our Universe. If we cry we are attended to. It becomes the norm that whatever we need comes. As we get older the world does not revolve around us and in protest we throw tantrums. Tantrums are our way of saying "Hey what the heck is going on here? I never requested a change in the status quo. Can't you see I have needs that aren't being met?" Well of course as you evolve out of childhood, you take yourself to the bathroom and you show up or orchestrate your own meals. All of this "having to do" hits a child like a lead balloon as it is antithetical to how it has been up to now.

The next fly in the ointment is that as we get older we are given more and more boundaries and conditions that we have to live up to in order to get what we want. Therefore, we naturally come to believe that if we obey these boundaries we will be honored and get the love that we want and need. Hence this is the beginning of our looking outside rather than in for validation and feeling worthwhile, let alone loved. However, there is no one around to tell us that we also live in a moderate to severe dysfunctional family. And that the parents we believe to be of a divine order aren't. Now here's where it really gets tricky. If we are doing what we are supposed to do and the divine parents don't come through with the supportive and emotional goodies, then we have two choices: 1) we can cave into hopelessness and depression; or 2) we can keep hope alive by blaming ourselves and "trying" harder.

The survival-oriented thing to do is to implement option number two (the trying perspective is described in an earlier chapter). So as we blame ourselves year after year, we hold at a core subconscious psychological DNA level a learned sense of poor self-esteem due to taking on a job that is not possible to succeed at. Hence, we focus on getting our validation and acceptance from those we turn over our power over to, i.e., our parents looking outside of our selves for personal affirmation. This coupled with Western society's teaching that worth and credibility are acquired from the outside reinforces goals that are paradoxical to centering, autonomy, empowerment, and health.

The last twist to this complex situation is that society at large has a major investment in socializing everyone to the notion that how you are perceived and valued comes from the outside. From Hollywood to New York, who you know and how you are seen is everything. Obviously all of our magazines advertising fashion, looks, presentation, and therefore acceptance are up for grabs with each issue. It is understandable that all of this is marketing in a commercial, capitalistic, materialistic society, but what is not okay is that instead of just a preference on how you want to look it gets connoted as a barometer of acceptance.

The perfect movie depicting this [as you know I love using movies as examples as they are fiction imitating life] is *The*

Devil Wears Prada. In this movie not only is the fashion magazine an icon of what is acceptable to be seen in and ones' worth, but also competence and professionalism are second to presentation. This movie is perfect for reinforcing that character, stability, integrity, honesty, and a centered sense of self just don't count. Unfortunately, our Western society and even much of the world basis too much on this principle. One-upmanship is not an idea, an action, or a concept; it's a way of life. It is a lifestyle that reinforces that we are to look and desire what the outside thinks of us not the in.

CLIENT: *I have been thinking about what you said about owning my truth. It is clearer to me that I do look for others to tell me how I am doing and what is ok. I would like to change that.*

DR. R.: *Yes as long as you take your cues on how you are doing in the world you will be like a willow bending whichever way the wind blows.*

CLIENT: *Yes that is how it feels. I am never at peace with who I am and anyone can wreck my day with a criticism.*

DR. R.: *So when has there been a time recently that you had an epiphany or "a-ha" moment that resonated in your body not in your head.*

CLIENT: *Well, I did have a situation at work where for some reason I knew that a certain decision had to be made and there was no time to wait.*

DR. R.: *Exactly. That is what I am talking about and you are feeling it exactly where one's truth resonates. It is always in the body not in the intellect in a manner that is specific and clear.*

CLIENT: *Yes it was like that. I wanted to second-guess it but it was so strong a feeling I could not ignore it.*

DR. R.: *Again, exactly. It is a resounding feeling that is not to be ignored and you know not think it. In fact one of the ways to assure yourself that this is the right feeling besides the resonance you feel, is that your mind will want to debate it and talk you out of it.*

CLIENT: *Yea that's right. I remember my thoughts going off like bells attempting to get me to reconsider.*

DR. R.: *Yes, your mind is logical and your feeling/truth is not. The mind goes crazy over the lack of data that your truth wants to act on. The mind does not feel safe or secure with what it believes is impulsive actions. It wants data and lots of it.*

CLIENT: *Yes that is what it felt like. As if my mind wanted to have a confrontation and out debate what I truly felt in all my being was the right way to move.*

DR. R.: *The mind wants to bring the heavy guns of logic and linear thinking to offset what it cannot understand, which is the intangible. So when the debate engages you know that your mind is baulking at the truth's sense of what to do. This lets you know you are in your truth.*

CLIENT: *So this debate gives me a heads up that my mind is trying to talk me out of my own true sense of what to do.*

DR. R.: *As strange as that sounds, yes. Our truth comes from something that is intangible but from our higher sense of our path. The mind, like the ego, does not like this nor does it want to be second-guessed. And yet as you said, when you know the truth as it resonates in your being there is not another way to go.*

Now the next thing I would like you to do is can you feel what that resonance vibrated like in your body and where it did.

CLIENT: *Yes if I check inside I can get a sense of that.*

DR. R.: *Good. Now I want you to memorize the feeling of that vibration and where it is in your body because it will always feel like that and come from that place in your body. Whether you are making a decision on what to eat or a major decision at work, your truth will ring in this way. And only when it does vibrate in this manner and in that place in your body will it be the truth.*

CLIENT: *This is very weird.*

DR. R.: *I know. The intangible is not something our mind is comfortable with. Hence, there will be times that your truth will ring in this way and your mind will convince you to ignore it.*

This is the trial and error learning that we all must go through in learning to trust our inner truth. This learning takes some time so be gentle on your self. There will be times that you listen and the reinforcement will be there and so too when you don't listen. As you get more trusting and comfortable with the outcome, you will walk in your inner self and validate what is so for you.

CLIENT: *This is exciting and I am looking forward to getting there.*

DR. R.: *It is that and you will.*

The best example of this is the Biblical story of The Prodigal Son. In this story, one of two sons goes off to the "far country." He decides to take his money and go off to investigate and indulge in the world. His brother decides to stay home with his father who he hopes will be appreciative, and love him more. The prodigal son goes further and further into the "far country" where rules and limits don't exist and people indulge themselves by acting out and superficial behaviors. He stays in this environment for many years to his own detriment. After years of riotous living he has lost himself to such a degree that he is living in literal swill. It is at this moment of hitting bottom that he realizes how empty he feels and that he wants to be whole and healthy, and begins to pick himself up and look for the road home. Since at this time he is so lost and without an inner sense of direction, he struggles with how to proceed. As he braves this struggle and pushes on further down the journey, his father comes out to meet him. This is symbolic of our own journey, which commences out of being sick and tired of hitting the same unfulfilling wall. We know as we hit bottom, i.e., living in swill that either who we are is going to perish or we must take the first step toward our inner salvation.

As we brave this, as we are not sure of the direction, we begin to get glimpses of the path. As we show the Universe that we are walking our talk and being in truth, out higher self/our inner divine comes out to meet and guide us. Like the Prodigal son's father comes out to take him the rest of the way home. Home in this analogy is our own center where however you refer to it; the soul, the witness, our higher self, or our wisdom begins to welcome us home to our inner divine self. It begins to offer us insights that we use to have access to and lost. In essence we never really lost them, but we became lost to them as we prioritized the "far country" hence the outside rather than our inside depth of awareness and clarity of truth.

My friend Dr. Rick Moss likens this to an analogy of the light and the lampshade. He says that our internal divine light is always there, but it is shaded from us and we have learned to identify with the lampshade. I like this analogy because it aptly identifies the issue I am pointing out. We get so caught up in our miss-beliefs of self, thinking we are the outer container that we get outer-directed not inner. We see other lampshades, which we envy and want to emulate, or do whatever it takes to have "one like them." What makes matters worse is that we react to the others' lampshades, unable to see their inner light.

This leads to everyone reacting from the ego, setting up scenarios that have more to do with inappropriate actions and judgments than learning our lessons. It perpetuates competition, fuels feelings of being unsupported and alone. If everyone could come from the perspective of the light, then we could witness each other's learning process and offer support and guidance, rather than one-upmanship or belittling. Hence, caught up in the script and the play and not being able to own the perspective of the witness in the audience.

It is this journey back towards the self where we can reclaim the essence of who we are and be in our truth. We are so entrenched and socialized to believe that the way to our salvation is through others acceptance. We are told that credibility and worth are about tangible/material things. It is not that toys are bad or are not fun to own, but they are not our identity. One's identity can only be found from the inside where the "I" lives. We can have lots of pleasures and diversions, but we must not believe for a moment that they are anything more than a wonderful outside distraction. If you want to feel value, worth, and to know who you are; look inside.

When we drop into consciousness, we are not at the whim of emotions and negative self-image, which only keep us chasing an outside illusion of well-being. The pursuance of this outside illusion which keeps us hoping that our salvation and heightened self-actualization can come about from outside ourselves is true folly. It gives rise to what are the two major saboteurs of any chance we have at personal abundance and success: Trying and Shoulds.

CHAPTER 5

TRYING & SHOULDS – THE LANGUAGE OF FAILURE

This next part is going to sound like psychobabble semantics, but I assure you it is anything but. These are two of the biggest contributors to the mental trash bin that we carry, and the ongoing sabotage of our getting "there." Over many years of listening to people broach the subject matter of pursuing goals, they will use the words "should" or "trying" rather than the more empowered terms of "wanting" and "doing." I kept being taken back by the number of times clients would use these terms during a session with regard to themselves or their spouse/partner.

I also began to see a connection between adult children of alcoholics, rageaholics, and children of narcissistic parents with the words *should* and *trying*. It became apparent to me that this was not about an act of doing or actually accomplishing, but an unconscious inner child dynamic of waiting and sabotaging. This unconscious need to stay stuck was about wanting to be heard, honored, cherished, valued, or loved in a way that these dysfunctional parents could never offer or accommodate. Here again is a powerful miss-belief that we have no inner personal power and that we must control our lives and in fact our destiny from the outside in.

This may sound contradictory to how we believe life works, but it is not...this is backwards thinking as to how our process works, and only causes us to end up feeling a sense of dread, hopelessness, and depression. The mix up occurs in childhood, when instinctively we expect parents to be divine mother and father. However, with seriously dysfunctional parents/caregivers who are more like impenetrable non-responding walls than nurturers, this does not happen, as dysfunctional is not divine. No matter what we need, feel or want, with dysfunctional parents it is like a tree falling in the woods with no one there to hear it. Being children who have no one to tell us how dysfunctional and non-divine our parents/caregivers truly are, we do the next natural thing to keep hope in our survival alive: we blame ourselves.

Thus as children, we can't venture into the idea that our parents are too damaged to attend to us; it's just too hopeless. In order to keep the hope alive that we have a chance of being attended to, we take on the burden/blame that it is <u>us</u> who are not saying or doing it correctly. So we keep *shoulding* on our selves and *trying* to get through an impenetrable wall hoping to be heard, honored, cherished, and loved.

Let's first take the word *trying*. It is to attempt, not achieve. Therefore the more we *try*, by definition, the more we fail. All this while we keep re-inventing different methods to get through to the gods in our lives, i.e., parents who could never hear us in the first place. And if that weren't bad enough we keep taking on the onus that it must be our fault. As this goes on through our childhood we internalize a subconscious miss-belief that we are not able to achieve or get through anywhere, and have made the failure of *trying* a lifestyle. Hence, always *trying* to be heard, *trying* to be honored, *trying* to be appreciated, *trying* to be cherished and *trying* to be included, while in constant amazement that it never works and we never succeed.

Even more so as adults we take on the failure of the behavior as if we are the ones not doing the right thing. If you believe you are trying but not succeeding then it becomes your problem to resolve. This perspective puts the blame on the individual *trying*. The one delivering the message must not be doing it correctly; therefore the object of their communication is not at fault for not receiving appropriately. Hence, the one who is to receive the message is not wrong nor has any ownership of the problem. Only when one's work is further along does the patient realize that all along they <u>have</u> been saying what is so for them, but the person they are directing it to has <u>no</u> availability to hear them.

As I work with people in psychotherapy, this issue of *trying* insidiously shows up in their vocabulary no matter whom they are talking about. They are constantly referring to ways in which they are not heard, honored, validated, appreciated, cherished, or let in. They are always inferring that they are failing to get through to the other person as they keep *trying*. A typical example of this would be:

CLIENT: *I was trying to tell my wife that I wanted her to look at how she organizes her time and the stress that results from that.*

DR. R.: *What happened as you did this?*

CLIENT: *She got angry with me for bringing this up and causing her to be more stressed.*

DR. R.: *What did you do as she got angry?*

CLIENT: *I got really mad but I held it in and tried to get her to realize that I was not trying to hurt her but help.*

DR. R.: *Then what happened?*

CLIENT: *She got more upset with me and told me I had no idea how to help and walked out of the room.*

DR. R.: *Did you notice how often you used the word "trying" in your explanations to me?*

CLIENT: *No.*

DR. R.: *You used the word "tried" or "trying" about three or four times. This may sound like semantics, but "trying" is the language of failure.*

CLIENT: *[looking confused] I don't see how that is.*

DR. R.: *In many years of practice I have learned that "trying" is the language of a little child whose parents won't hear him and he keeps "trying" to be heard. That there is no one to tell him that his parents are like this wall behind me (I sit with a chair against a wall of my office and I take my open hand and tap it against the wall showing it is not going to give way or bend) and that no matter how you run against it, it will not let you through to the other office. That you can run at it or walk, use you shoulder or your behind, have padding or not, and it will not give way.*

CLIENT: *My parents were not ones who would listen to what was going on with me. I always just went to my room and stayed by myself. If I did say something bothered me, my father who was drinking would ignore me and my mother would give me food.*

DR. R.: *Yes, your father was emotionally anesthetized and your mother did what she knew to nurture and feed your pain. Neither of them knew how to step in and talk to you about what you were feeling and you blamed yourself for not being respond-ed to. And when you own that it's your fault that they did not respond, you keep looking for how you could have done it better believing you are doing it badly, hence failing.*

CLIENT: *Yes, you're right. I do keep wondering what I am do-ing wrong and trying to do it right. Oh, I said trying again.*

DR. R.: *Yes you did and it again speaks to how you are failing. Once you realize that you are not "trying" to talk to the person,* *but are saying what you want to say, you will see where the other person has the responsibility of stepping up too. For instance, you are letting your wife know that you believe she is not organizing things well and upping her stress. She does not want to hear it and gets angry with you or walks out when you bring it up.*

CLIENT: *You're right. She doesn't want to discuss it.*

DR. R.: *Yes, she does not and it has nothing to do with your communication. Once you get that you can confront her on not wanting to talk with you about this, the doors of communication have a better chance of opening. And if she refuses, in not blaming yourself you can make decisions from that point as to how to proceed with her.*

The most revealing aspect of this exchange is the realization that the client is not doing anything particularly wrong. He is bringing up a conflict that the wife does not want to deal with for her own reasons pertaining to her subconscious miss-beliefs. Once he sees that he is stepping up, not *trying*, he begins to lighten up on himself and feels less helpless. He begins to see that he is making sense and can hold others (in this case, his wife) accountable for what they won't deal with, while giving himself credit for stepping up and communicating his needs with his partner.

Thus, if you believe you are inadequate at communicating and not getting through to others, you will self-prophesize this wherever you go. Once you realize that it is not you who is failing and therefore dismantle your miss-belief, you will not let others run you away or get by not answering. All of a sudden, you find that you are holding people accountable and having successful dialogues with them. This win-win situation from one had always been about losses and lack of resolve. Your self-esteem goes up as you own your actions, while giving others their responsibility for <u>not</u> stepping up.

Second, let's take on the cousin to *trying* which is the concept of "should." *Shoulds* are almost always other peoples' expectations or demands on us with regard to gaining respect and being loved. It comes up frequently and is coupled with the *trying* which goes hand in hand with conditionally loving homes. "Shoulding" on yourself perpetuates the idea that you are inadequate and not living up to expectations set down by those who formulate the parameters of your acceptance.

Examples of *shoulds,* a la outside expectations are:

You Should (or Shoulds):

Keep trying	Not rock the boat
Rescue	Not have an opinion
Be the peacemaker	Keep feelings to yourself
Stay quiet	Not be lazy
Listen to their problems	Be happy
Not be a burden	Not have needs
Know what to do	Not ask for help
Take care of "us"	Not have your feelings

Anticipate beyond your years	Make my/our lives happy
Make us proud	Make our lives better
Keep our image in the community	Never settle
Keep our secrets	Be the parent
Be more	Honor thy parents-even if…
Read everyone's mind	Not expect too much
Be perfect	Always be in control
Always be fine	

You hopefully do not identify with all of these, but the ones that do resonate with you are holding you back. These learned, outside-of-self expectations are there for only one purpose: to make you feel less than.

Of course, all families have degrees of this and that is normal. In the course of a lifetime or during our formative years, we will, as a mentor of mine used to say, "should on ourselves." Thus, we all need to be cognizant of putting this on ourselves, especially those who grew up in more severely dysfunctional homes. These include substance issues or rage that make *shoulding* on yourself a family tradition. It is here that one must be more aware and counter *shoulds* with a redirect to one's heart. It is in the heart that we know what it is that we want. *Shoulds* are only others' expectations that leave us feeling lazy, lost, stupid, procrastinating, unproductive, and eventually hopeless.

This is because *shoulds* are other peoples' expectations of us, which means they are not ours. It is not truly what we want to do and we are tired of proving our worth to get love and honoring. Only by bringing *shoulds* to an inner "want" can we truly get a sense of ownership and knowing whom we really are and what we really want to do. If it turns out we do want to do whatever "it" is, then we will without hesitation or stumbling step up and do it. Our actions won't contain hesitation, procrastination, half attempts, or be done without resolve. To accomplish this, every time you put a *should* on yourself, which as I said is an outside expectation, take the sense of it being outside yourself and bring it to your heart.

What I mean is imagine taking the outside *should* as a tangible entity and literally bring it into your chest and place it on your heart. Then ask yourself if this is something that feels right and what you want to do. If it resonates, then go on, but if not, let it go. An example would be if you like and want to work at your job, but there is paperwork you don't want to do. Bring the issue of your job to your heart and though you may moan about the paperwork do you want to complete the paperwork because you want to keep the job? If you find yourself procrastinating on all aspects of your job, when you bring the question of whether you really want to do it to your heart the answer will probably be no. This is an example of a session on *shoulds*:

CLIENT: *I know there are many things I should be taking care of but I just can't find the time to do them.*

DR. R.: *What does that make you think in terms of yourself?*

CLIENT: *What do ya think? I feel stupid and lazy, and that I am always letting people down.*

DR. R.: *What does that feel like?*

CLIENT: *I told you I feel like I am a failure and a loser.*

DR. R.: *Is it that you never get anything accomplished?*

CLIENT: *Well, no. There are a lot of things that I take on at work or in my shop that come out pretty well if I do say so myself.*

DR. R.: *What is the difference in the things you procrastinate on and those you complete well?*

CLIENT: *That's a good question. I don't know.*

DR. R.: *Is there anything that comes to mind that feels different to you about the two scenarios?*

CLIENT: *Nothing other than at home I feel there are things that I should be doing for my family or that I feel guilty about.*

DR. R.: *Yes, that is correct. A mentor of mine used to say "don't should on your self."*

CLIENT: *[Laughs] That's a good one. I can see that I should on myself a lot.*

DR. R.: *Yes, I have heard you use the word many times while we have been talking. Shoulds are expectations of what others want from us and are rarely what we want for ourselves.*

CLIENT: *You know Doc, I have done that most of my life. I was brought up to live up to my families' expectations and not really think about what is important to me.*

DR. R.: *I am not saying that you will not want to do for your family, but when our self worth is on the line then we look at what others want as a way to be loved. Therefore, you will procrastinate on what you feel is about acceptance and complete those you want to be successful at.*

CLIENT: *I never realized how true that is. So I am not lazy?*

DR. R.: *No you are not lazy and in fact I don't believe in the word lazy. It is always a representation of some deeper underlying issue. I think you will be surprised that when you are not shoulding on yourself, you will see how much more you complete. When we should on our selves it is like a big stick beating us up, only resulting in being bloody and depressed. There is no learning or growth from that.*

CLIENT: *[Smiling] I get it.*

I ask my clients and I will ask you also to be watchful of the many times you use *trying* and *should* around your relationships, goals and objectives. I hope you do not still think of this as psychobabble semantics, but the more you eradicate these terms from your vocabulary you will be amazed at the energy you bring to owning and completing your objectives. It seems so simple, but it is a major contributor to the subconscious trash we carry into our daily lives causing delays and poor follow through. It is also a major contributor to enabling our miss-beliefs that cause sabotage and failure in our lives by believing through an inappropriately empowering that we actually have control over how and where our life goes. This too causes us to sabotage our future due to a heightened sense of entitlement and fairness.

CHAPTER 6

THE ILLUSION OF CONTROL

This chapter looks at the miss-belief that we carry regarding the illusion that we are in control. We believe that in Western society we can make things happen exactly as we want. What's interesting is that there is a fallacy as well as truth to this.

The fallacy is that we can control life. This very notion of control is not only arrogant but a misnomer. This is highlighted in a scene from the movie *Instinct* with Anthony Hopkins and Cuba Gooding Jr. In the scene I am referring to Anthony Hopkins puts Cuba Gooding Jr. through a rough ordeal in order to teach him that control is only an illusion. We believe and it is reinforced that we can bend the world or others to our will, and that they are somehow at the mercy of our power. Hmmm, where have I heard this before, oh yea, American Capitalism. If life is anything, it is basically unpredictable and the only control we have is to bring all of who we are to every situation. The truth about having control is only with hard work and the right intention can we hope to produce that which we want.

Control is therefore not over others, the work place, our relationships, the environment, or anything that is outside of us. The control we have is to go inside and attend to our deepest places of unrest, insecurity, and shadow. It is from this place that we can become our purist self: projecting intentions into the quantum field and have the self-fulfilling prophecy of matter interact with our being. The Universe is ready and willing to give an equal and positive reaction to our intention. This is the law of physics. It is from here that all that we want and desire will appear. And every time we go outside of our selves to impact something tangible or some other person from our own egoistic state, we lose.

I believe it was Eleanor Roosevelt who said, "No one can make you feel inferior without your consent." Most people give up their right to self-influence. They do it out of insecurity, fear, anxiety, indecision, guilt, a dysfunctional need to be liked, or desperate need to make money. If we truly understood this concept, then we can reclaim our legitimate right to self-actualize by owning our actions and reactions.

Many of the people I work with will get to a point in their therapy where they will be on the precipice of what they all refer to as "losing control." For most this is fought with fear. It terrorizes them to the point that it is almost a life and death struggle. They will hold on to the point of almost not breathing so as not to go to the place in them selves that they were taught was *verboten* and completely unacceptable. My typical response is twofold: "What does that mean?" and "What would it look like if you did?"

An example of this is:

CLIENT: *I don't want to look at where we are headed.*

DR. R.: *We are headed toward your heart and the feelings that have been harbored there all your life.*

CLIENT: *Yea, well that is scary, as I don't want to lose control.*

DR. R.: *What does that mean and what would that look like?*

CLIENT: *Well, I would lose it and fall apart.*

DR. R.: *What do you mean lose "it?"*

CLIENT: *I would not be able to control myself.*

DR. R.: *When most of the people I work with say that what they mean is not that they won't be in control, but they will not be able to control and hold back their feelings.*

CLIENT: *Yea, that is what I mean.*

DR. R.: *What would be so awful if you dropped into your feelings?*

CLIENT: *What does that even mean?*

DR. R.: *When I say drop into your feelings what I mean is to go inside and ferret out how you are feeling. To go to a deeper level than you typically identify what is going on inside of you, like where you breathe and your soul lives. To go to the place that is beyond what you usually conceive as feeling and where your brain just comes up with I don't know. What goes on for you when I say all of this?*

CLIENT: *I don't really know but it scares me to think about it.*

DR. R.: *So many of us are brought up to believe that feelings are unacceptable, ugly, weak, and to be walked away from.*

CLIENT: *That is how I was taught to see them. If I brought up any feelings that were negative, someone would get after me. Or it would look like I hurt or disappointed them.*

DR. R.: *Yes. You, like many others, were taught that if you showed the tough feelings you would be bad, mean, or insensitive.*

CLIENT: *Yea that is how it was.*

DR. R.: *In this you learned to "control" your feelings so that you would not be considered bad or unacceptable. Hence not be loved.*

CLIENT: *I never quite looked at it that way.*

DR. R.: *Feelings do not need to be controlled and you are not out of control if you feel them or let them out. It is how you were* *trained. If you go to a comedy club and hear a comedian, you laugh. Well if you are sad or angry it is just as normal to cry or get heated.*

CLIENT: *I really never saw that it was natural. You are right. In my house it was really not ok to show how you felt. I did learn that control meant to shut myself down so that they would not have to deal with me.*

DR. R.: *Right. You learned that staying in control was a way not to be rejected and unloved. You shut you down at the expense of "you" so that "they" could stay in their system of denial and dysfunction.*

CLIENT: *I get it (it is often with this new insight at a deeper level that the person will start to cry or look very somber as years of suppression start to come to the surface. It is this surfacing that allows substantive healing.)*

There is an old Yiddish saying: "Man plans, God laughs." The more we attempt to make things go our way, i.e., be in control, the more those plans go awry or not at all. As shown above, we learn this process in our family systems to suppress our feelings. This is not to say that doing our homework and working hard does not pay off, but as the other old saying goes, work smart not hard. People who work very hard without the right intentioning, planning and orchestration fall short of what they want. They are typically frustrated, angry people who are forever shouting to the heavens why are things are so hard? They see others getting the fruits of their labor and rail at the Universe for the unfairness they are suffering. These people are in their way and subconsciously sabotaging their own progress due to unfelt wounds in their psyche. This sabotage or acting out behavior is the subconscious' need to be controlling and override our day-to-day conscious goals and wants. <u>This is due to unresolved insecurities and wounds that don't believe we have a right to be valued or found worthy.</u>

As I stated in both my books, it is the subconscious that projects control over us. The only way to reclaim our selves and become empowered is to unlearn the "learned personality" and eradicate the knee jerk reactions caused by our psychological wounds. I am not going to go into the specifics of this as you can read it in my book, *The Road To Me: Reclaiming Your Power*. But if you think this is psychobabble, was there ever a time you thought you had put something negative in your personality behind you, and it showed up again sabotaging your success? This sabotage or acting out behavior is the subconscious' need to be controlling and overriding our day-to-day conscious goals and wants.

One example would be if you are in a relationship with someone who is demeaning you and telling you that you are never good enough. It is the hope that after the end of this type of relationship you say to yourself, "I have learned my lesson and I will never do that again." Yet you meet someone down the road and at first the person seems to be completely different and could never be like your last relationship. Unfortunately six months or a year later you find you are with only a slightly better version of what you had before. In absolute amazement you hit your head and say, "How did this happen?" This is how the subconscious need of proving your self to someone who could never honor you is in control and takes priority over your conscious desire to have a healthy relationship. As long as your family of origin's subconscious miss-belief of self holds the learned personalities sense of being "less than," you will continue to find this type of relationship until you unlearn this.

We believe that in order to control our business we have to keep our foot on the pulse of our production or/and on the necks of our employees. Though this does have impact, productivity and morale on this level will clearly over time, deteriorate. Whatever results you may be getting, even if they are good, there is more to be had. Working at a level of empowerment, facilitating good will, and respect along with firm boundaries and goals will take you to the top of the mountain. It is the very essence of teamwork and groupthink that all the industrial literature talks about.

We have been brought up with the mentality that control is essential, with the philosophy that might makes right. It looks like this perspective works if you don't factor in back biting, passive-aggressive sabotage, unethical practices, disloyalty, mistrust, substance abuse, affairs, feelings of isolation, dis-ease, and premature death. What looks like success is just the old way of doing things, and does not mean it's the best and only way to do that thing. We vie for control because it is safer than having to be vulnerable and honest. We hold a miss-belief that "nice guys finish last" and that vulnerability is for suckers who invoke a personal or professional death.

Every ten years, knowing there must be a better way than old fashioned control, the business community entertains another philosophical ideology to reframe the way corporations work. In the seventies it was offering help for Occupational Burnout; in the eighties it was mirroring the Japanese corporate style of a family and in the nineties they called it Corporate Soul. None of these lasted because it is too scary for American corporations to embrace something so real, honest and trusting. If they weren't able to govern in fear, CEOs would not know how to lead. They are still working under the old premise, (miss-belief) that they would not have the respect or control they deserve and need to run a successful company.

What this truly breeds are work environments that are full of deceit, theft, toxicity, personal contempt, substance abuse, and a deep inner sense of being lost, alone, and profoundly empty. This is the stuff that mid-life crises are made of. Only from this male miss-belief could the ridiculous and delusional bumper sticker depicting mass rationalization be created: "He who dies with the most toys wins." As I have said before, it would seem to me that all this implies is that someone <u>rich is dead</u>. It reminds me of the joke that upon reaching the Pearly Gates, St. Peter never heard a CEO proclaim, "I should have stayed longer at the office."

The sad thing about believing the miss-belief that we are in control of our lives is that it keeps us pushing the envelope to make the river flow the direction we want it to.

It means that instead of going inside to where we really own personal control we continue to look outside of ourselves for the answer. In thinking we control our world, we look outside into the world for our relief. This does no one any good, perpetuates the difficult times we are facing, while offering no relief. From this perspective, we eventually fall into a learned helplessness leading to depression. Again here is a miss-belief that we have no personal inner power and that we are not the designer of our lives.

This may sound contradictory but it is not. Outside of our selves is where we are taught to negotiate life. It is to outside worth and validation we go to feel accepted and good about our selves. It then stands to reason that we look outside of our selves to gain control. This is backwards, and only causes us to end up in a place of helplessness or depression. It is the illusion that has no real basis in reality. It is only from the inside that we are able to affect the quantum field of the Universe, intentioning that which will provide us with what we want. Our control is only inside of ourselves where we have the power to impact our lives.

The truth regarding having some kind of control lies within us at the subconscious level. It is where we have to clean up the trash bin and replace it with healthy, good beliefs. Again as my friend, Dr. Rick Moss says, 'if you want to know what you want, look at what you have.' This comes from the perspective that we intention from our subconscious exactly what we believe the Universe will give us. If your miss-belief at the subconscious level is that you are not deserving of being loved or cherished, then as long as this exists no matter how many relationships you have been in or how mature you are, you will still end up with an upgraded though familiar version of an unloving partner, attempting to prove your right to be loved. Therefore, we must go into the inner psyche and do our emotional healing so that there is no impediment (controlling miss-belief) overriding our truest and healthiest desires.

As I stated in my first book, there is no short cut to this. Our inner work is our inner work. You would not expect to do a physical workout once or read a fitness book and feel the process is complete. Not only that, but the bad news is to stay in shape you have to discipline yourself to work out forever; so too, with our emotional health. One must get to it, figure it out and then stay with this endeavor of expanding inner consciousness and insight. This is our inner work and can even be called our spiritual practice as it does lead to wisdom. This work puts us in touch with our core sense of truth, which is a barometer that never lies to us and from which intentioning, manifests.

Now, as you may have read or seen either *What the #$*! do we (k)now!?*, or *The Secret* this is where our ability to consciously control originates, i.e. intentioning. As I mentioned above, the Bible talks about it by saying, as you believe it so is it done unto you, and the Buddhists say, it will be given to you, as you believe it. Wayne Dyer has a book entitled, *You'll See it When You Believe It*, and again my sense is that the subconscious need will override the conscious want.

All of these give the same message; that we are in the quantum field of the "One" and everything begets everything.

Therefore, if we project a true need, one that is not from our egoistic state, into the abundant field of the Universe, quantum physics dictates that a self-prophesizing and equal reaction will return to us. Those of us who believe in the Universe, a phenomenon that is beyond this mortal plane, know that there is a synergy awaiting us with the abundance we are seeking.

What short circuits this is thinking, intellectualizing and projecting from a cerebral orientation, or from the denial world of the subconscious. The only result from this perspective is a headache. This is why so many people who want to believe and attempt what intentioning is all about give up after "trying" once or a hundred times. No matter how many times you drink from a muddy glass the results will still be mud. Only a glass of pure water is able to quench your thirst. And only intentioning from our purist sense of self is going to be in harmony with the Universe and bring us what we desire.

Therefore, we have to do the unlearning of the "learned personality" to take out the trash of our miss-beliefs that are sabotaging us from the depths of our selves and wrongly controlling us. Once this is unlearned, then we can access who we are at our truest essence and be empowered to bring about that which we want-and get it. This empowerment comes from the realization that we must always work from the inside out of self to bring all of who we are to the moment.

There is a reference in the Old Testament where Moses asks how shall he identify or name God, and God answers,

"I Am Who I Am." As I so often refer to this Shakespearean quote, 'To thine own self be true.' Additionally, when you are in your own truth and come from the depths of that you will not fall into the trap of making assumptions, which are almost never right and only cause havoc.

CHAPTER 7

ASSUMPTIONS

One of the worst miss-beliefs that need to be trashed is around the issue of assumptions. Assumptions are the easy, inappropriate short cut to figuring out why something is the way it is or why someone is acting toward you in a particular manner. To anyone who has lived inside Corporate America or experienced couples therapy, assumptions are the mother of all sabotage. Those who have been in corporate seminars or couples work have seen assume broken down into ass-u-me (this stands for making an ass out of you and me). Anytime you leap to an assumption you will probably be wrong and behave incorrectly because of it. Why? Because if you act on an assumption as if it's true regarding someone or some company's process, you are very likely to get it wrong. The only thing to do with your assumption is to check it out and see if it stands up to scrutiny. You may be absolutely correct with regard to your assumption, but if you do not check it out you will more times than not end up face down in the dirt. In the corporate world, this could mean your job or a severe loss of respect, status, or money.

In a committed relationship/marriage, assumptions can mean anything from a strong disagreement to divorce depending on how often and for how long they occur.

The problem here is twofold: the first is discussed above, and the second is when we assume, we tend to act as if the company or the person is the assumption we are making up. Now without my going into a detailed account since it is obvious why not to do this, oh but wait just in case it's not so obvious, let me go into more detail. The reason to beat this concept into the ground or our heads is because assumptions keep happening. EVERYWHERE.

You really would think with all the consultants and marriage therapists harping on why not to do this, it would stop. But NO, it keeps happening. So what happens as you treat companies or significant others or spouses as if they are your assumption? How about losing a huge deal because you treated or approached your strategy or business plan based on your assumption not the company's reality? How about resentment due to the disrespect and disconnection the other person feels as you dealt with them as if they were your assumption?

The bad part of this as you can see is that we hold our assumptions to be real or true, when they are not. They are our own conjecture of what we believe is going on, how we will be dealt with, or in some way treated in the future. It is a bad offense to a concerned defense. It comes from wanting to be in control, wanting to protect our selves, not wanting to be caught off guard, not wanting to be hurt, wanting to be right, etc. It is amazing how our egos need to be on top, while getting the jump on catastrophe or needing to be the hero. It is so ingrained in our Western capitalist society and the subconscious that we don't even see it as wrong or inappropriate. It is just an accepted part of surviving.

Here's how it can show up in a committed relationship as well as making it apparent how men and women process differently:

WIFE: *We are unable to communicate without getting into a verbal conflict. Every time I try to tell him something he gets bossy and treats me like I am one of his employees.*

DR. R.: *How does he treat you?*

WIFE: *Well, I approach him with some problem going on at work and he immediately goes into this search and rescue mission. He asks me all sorts of questions and then goes right into not only answering them but telling me how to handle it.*

DR. R.: *How does that make you feel?*

WIFE: *Like asking him who the hell he thinks he is or never approaching him again.*

DR. R.: *Yes that is how you are thinking and what action you want to take, but how are you feeling about his approach?*

WIFE: *I feel angry and incredibly disrespected like he thinks I am an idiot who can't succeed or think without his divine intervention.*

DR. R.: *What do you think about what you wife is saying and feeling?*

HUSBAND: *Look Doc, if she doesn't want my opinion then she shouldn't ask for it.*

DR. R.: *Where in the scenario that she just laid out did she ask for your opinion?*

HUSBAND: *Well, she came to me and wanted to tell me what was going on, and how to deal with it.*

DR. R.: *Did she?*

HUSBAND: *Well you heard her.*

DR. R.: *Did you ask your husband at any time for his opinion on the issue?*

WIFE: *NO, I never do.*

DR. R.: *In John Gray's <u>Men Are from Mars, Women Are from Venus</u> he says that woman have a propensity to use "always" and "never." Do you mean "never" or "most of the time" because men will take you at your words and take issue with that.*

WIFE: *Well, in that case most of the time.*

HUSBAND: *Yes, she does that a lot and I do get defensive that I don't do things all the time.*

DR. R.: *These issues are common in couples and it might be good for you both to get the book or the DVD and read or watch it together. I often recommend this and to stop occasionally and discuss various issues that are brought up that related to your marriage.*

So what do you think when your wife says she rarely asks you to problem solve her issues?

HUSBAND: *What does she want because I assume that she is coming to me for help?*

DR. R.: *First off, assumptions are the mother of all screw-ups. When you assume something, you are running it through your own experiences or computer of what is. Most of the time you are wrong since you are looking at the issue through your own lenses instead of your partner's. You must check them out to make sure of what you believe because if you don't then you treat the other person as if they are behaving as you assume. From this perspective you will get it wrong and engage the other incorrectly and get anger or resentment back.*

So what is it that you are looking for from your husband because he is clueless and acting out from his assumptions?

WIFE: *I want to be able tell him about my day as well as be able to talk to him about things that bother me.*

DR. R.: *So you aren't looking for him to solve your problems?*

WIFE: *No, I can solve my own problems and as I said, it makes me feel like he thinks I am an idiot.*

HUSBAND: *Honey, you know I think you're very smart. I really don't know what to do here.*

WIFE: *If I want your help, I'll ask for you to problem solve this with me or just give me your thoughts on it.*

HUSBAND: *Doc, you got to help me out here. I still don't get what I am supposed to do.*

DR. R.: *Why don't you ask your wife?*

HUSBAND: *I don't know what you want. Help me out here.*

WIFE: *I need you to listen and be supportive.*

HUSBAND: *But that's not doing anything.*

WIFE: *Do you see what I am dealing with here, Dr. R.?*

DR. R.: *Yes, I see. What your wife is asking for is what is called empathy. It is where she feels she is able to get something off her chest with her partner and feel acknowledged and understood.*

HUSBAND: *I don't know if I can do that psychobabble stuff?*

DR. R.: *I know. As men we are asked to be linear;, have the answers, solve problems and move on.*

HUSBAND: *Yea, that I know how to do.*

DR. R.: *Well, how would you feel if you came home and told your wife that your manager was giving you problems and explained the situation and your wife told you how to handle it?*

HUSBAND: *I would lose it.*

DR. R.: *Right. You would not accept that from anyone nor would you like him or her for thinking you can't handle it.*

HUSBAND: *OK, if that's how you feel I get that part. But I still don't see how empathy is doing anything?*

WIFE: *I think I'll scream. I appreciate that you get how disrespectful it is but how can you be so smart and not get how it feels when someone supports you?*

DR. R.: *Women process their feelings. When a woman is dealing with something she calls up her friend and they talk for a time on the phone. When men are hurting they go off in a corner and only come out when they have got a handle on it. When women come to us to process their feelings it is because we are their partners and they want to relate to us. The relating part for us is to empathize which means we let them know that we are hearing them and get how they feel. It gives them a sense of support and being cared for.*

HUSBAND: *I understand it but I don't quite get it.*

DR. R.: *Would you be willing to role play a situation with your wife?*

HUSBAND: *What good would that do?*

DR. R.: *It will allow you to see how this works and experience your wife's different reaction to you. [to the wife] Would you be willing to attempt this?*

WIFE: *Yes*

DR. R.: *[Back to the husband] What do you think?*

HUSBAND: *[Reluctantly] OK.*

DR. R.: *OK. I would like you to pick a situation where you want your husband to listen and offer empathy to you.*

WIFE: *The other day my friend Stella got mad at me for not agreeing with her on an issue that came up with another friend of ours.*

HUSBAND: *Oh, I remember this. I wanted to help you see how Stella might have felt and why she would have reacted that way.*

WIFE [ANGRY]: *Yes you take her side and then totally lose how I feel or what is going on for me.*

HUSBAND: *That's not true. I was helping you to see both sides and work your friendship out.*

DR. R.: *Now you are in the content fight you often get into. It is where you [husband] are trying to fix it and get peace, and where you [wife] feel like he is siding with Stella and ignoring what you feel.*

HUSBAND AND WIFE: *Exactly.*

DR. R.: *[to the husband] What you are doing is the guy thing, that is taking ownership of getting the answer that makes you look good and smoothing over the controversy.*

HUSBAND: *What's wrong with that?*

DR. R.: *How's it working for you?*

HUSBAND: *It isn't.*

DR. R.: *Your wife is not saying she wants help solving the problem, nor is she asking you to make her friendship with Stella OK.*

HUSBAND: *Well then what is she asking for?*

DR. R.: *[to the wife] Can you tell him?*

WIFE: *I want you to listen to how Stella's attack hurt me and that I am sad that our friendship may not be able to continue.*

HUSBAND: *[Looking at Dr. Richman] What good will that do?*

DR. R.: *You mean what good will it do to have your wife feel that you care that she is hurting and that she is sad that her friendship is in crises?*

HUSBAND: *Oh, so how do I do this?*

DR. R.: *What you have to do is empathize, which means you need to give her the sense that you get she hurts and wish things were different.*

HUSBAND: *Like I keep saying, I have no idea how to do that.*

WIFE [LOOKING LIKE SHE COULD SCREAM]: *You see how hard it is for me to feel supported?*

HUSBAND: *But I do want her to feel that way.*

DR. R.: *I know. So I want you to say to her as psychobabble and UN-guy like as it sounds, I get that Stella maligned you and that you are stinging from it, and I wish I could make it stop.*

HUSBAND: *[Looking at his wife] What he said.*

DR. R.: *I know that would be easier, but I need you to practice.*

HUSBAND: *I understand that Stella hurt you and I wish there was more I could do to help.*

DR. R.: *[to the husband] Nicely done. [to the wife] How did that feel?*

WIFE: *It is what I needed.*

DR. R.[TO THE HUSBAND]: *It is not for you to fix it unless she asks for that kind of help. What she wants is to have an understanding that you hear she's in pain and are there to lean on when she is hurting.*

This is an example of how men and women are different and the many assumptions that get made on behalf of the difference. As John Gray points out in his book *Men Are from Mars, Women Are from Venus*, we are from different worlds and we need to communicate by clarifying the differences if we want to avoid a war. In the above scenario, most couples will get extremely annoyed at the other and end up in different parts of the house. I explain to couples that men go automatically to problem solve mode and women want to process things out, as well as need to be heard, listened to and empathized with. It is important to let each other know what you are wanting when initiating a conversation. If you do not do this, then assumptions will be made just due to the gender differences, let alone from the subconscious baggage we carry.

Again, the thing to look out for is that once we make an assumption, we then treat the other person as if our reality is the only possibility. This almost never works and will sooner than later cause havoc. Remember, our idiosyncrasies are our own and they need not be projected onto someone else.

An example of how Mars and Venus come into play is:

HUSBAND: *I feel constantly set up by her. She comes to me with something that she is dealing with and though my intention is to help all I get from her is that I am an ass.*

DR. R.: *So what is he doing that does not work for you?*

WIFE: *I come to him as my partner and I want him to listen to me.*

HUSBAND: *What? Not only do I listen but I am known in my company as someone who listens well and then offers a great strategy to go by.*

DR. R.: *I think that is the problem.*

HUSBAND: *I don't get it.*

DR. R.: *What is it that you are looking for when you talk about your situation?*

WIFE: *I want him to not only listen but give me the impression that he understands what I am going through.*

HUSBAND: *But that's not doing anything.*

DR. R.: *Actually, that's not true. She is asking for and needing your support and empathy.*

HUSBAND: *Right, I am not doing anything.*

WIFE: *Do you see, Dr. Richman, what I am dealing with??*

DR. R.: *Your wife does not need your intervention. She is more than bright enough to handle the situation.*

WIFE: *Yea.*

HUSBAND: *I know she is bright. It is one of the reasons I married her. All I want to do is help.*

DR. R.: *Yes, but you want to offer the Martian way of helping. You want to fix it and make it better, but that is in essence saying she can not handle it on her own.*

HUSBAND: *Is that what you feel?*

WIFE: *Yes. I don't need you to solve it, I can do that on my own. I need you to be there for me.*

HUSBAND: *I am always there for you.*

DR. R.: *You are physically there and caring, but woman, Venusians, want to be verbally supported and heard. And that is doing what they need. You don't have to get it or want that for you self, but that is what she needs. And if you want to give her what she needs, that's it.*

HUSBAND: *You're right I don't get it. But I can do it if that is what's called for.*

DR. R.: *That is what's called for. Most couples that don't get this start out where the wife comes to the husband and by the time Mars confronts Venus they are on opposite sides of the house.*

HUSBAND AND WIFE: *That is what happens.*

DR. R.: *If you can do this life will be better. Another thing to remember is when you approach the other to talk let the other know what it is you are asking for. Is it to be heard or problem solve?*

Another example of assumptions getting the better of us is:

HUSBAND: *I am here because she is always angry with me. Whenever she approaches, the way she asks me seems like she is waiting for me to say the wrong thing so she can go off on me.*

DR. R.: *As she begins to share with you, what does she do that triggers your assumption that she is out to get you?*

HUSBAND: *Her eyes are focused, her demeanor is harsh and she feels like she is in coiling mode ready to strike.*

DR. R.: *[turning to the wife] He assumes that every time you approach him you are angry. What do you think?*

WIFE: *I really don't know what to think. To listen to him I am this frightening monster and he is this weak lamb. I hear what he experiences and I want to ask him "Who are you living with?" because it can't be me.*

DR. R.: *What does go on for you when you need to ask him something or engage him in conversation?*

WIFE: *He is often extremely hard to engage. I feel like most of the times that I want to talk to him he gets distracted or just walks away. I never feel like I have his attention, or his presence, or eye contact. I just assume on my side that he does not want to talk to me or doesn't like me.*

DR. R.: *And how does that feel?*

WIFE: *Really hurtful and annoying.*

DR. R.: *Annoyance is one of the cousins of anger. So would it be fair to say that you might be angry because you experience an assumption that he will not want to engage when you approach?*

WIFE: *I see what you mean.*

DR. R.: *[turning to husband] And could it be that your wife is angry when she comes to talk because she feels you are constantly unavailable and not just because she is an angry woman out to get you?*

HUSBAND: *I didn't know I was hard to talk with. I am just always going and doing. I guess I never thought that she had to chase me down.*

WIFE: *What do you think I mean all the times that I tell you that I need you to connect and be present if I am going to talk to you?*

HUSBAND: *I just assumed you were trying to control me or stop me from what I needed to do, or what you didn't think was important.*

WIFE: *Why would I want to do that?*

DR. R.: *I would like you both to see that you were processing correctly but only from your own perspective. [Turning to husband] You were correct that she was angry and wanted you to stop and sit with her but not for the reason you thought. [Turning to wife] You were correct that he kept moving away and not giving you the appropriate attention but not because he did not want to talk to you. The problem is you both assumed the answer as to what you were experiencing in the other's behavior and never checked in to find out. Therefore, you both behaved toward the other as if your assumptions were true. This is always a recipe for disaster.*

As you will hear in any business or relationship seminar, assumptions are the mother of all screw-ups and missed perceptions. There is no truth or winning when you are living within your made up assumptions. All the answers in these situations lie in pursuing communication and clarity. The road to resolving and solving issues is to seek clarity regarding someone else's processing. As you seek clarity around someone else's processing you will be able to see them better and relate to them more truly. Thus relating to another in truth allows one to not assume or stereotype. Hence whatever differences one may have to another are not made out to be negative due to our own fears and insecurities, but are rather enjoyed for the natural difference they add.

CHAPTER 8

DIFFERENT AIN'T BAD

This chapter is not only about what is in your way of getting "there," that handcuffs us individually, but also has a threatening hold on our society and our human way of life. I am going to ask all of you to look at the fact that different is nothing more than that: different. It is the realistic fact that from the underwear you choose in the morning to the religion you worship will for the most part be different than the person who is standing, walking, sitting and existing on your left or on your right. It is my contention that different is a reality, the spice of life, but an inevitability that is here to stay. To try and buck it, fight it, or make it go away is as ludicrous as asking Detroit to make only one type of car with the same engine, same color, and body style. It would be ridiculous, and un-American to even ask for such a boring lack of choice.

Webster's college dictionary states that different is "not alike in character or quality; differing; dissimilar." In essence it is saying that different means there is dissimilarity in entities. Whether you are talking about objects, animals, people, genders, or races it is only that there is a difference, i.e., they are not the same. Hello. This difference is not by definition judged to be threatening, better or worse, good or bad.... only dissimilar. It means that there are qualities that one entity has that set it apart from the other. It means that every entity has its strengths and its limitations. I would like to believe this means that in and of itself each entity does not have all of the strengths to make a whole and definitive one. It might even mean that only when all entities are together in cooperation that then and only then will the strengths from that synergy combine to make a complete and perfect whole. Dare I suggest that it even creates oneness?

Yet many believe that different is something dangerous, fearful, threatening, and even against God's plan. That it is some sort of devilish plot and if we allow different to get too close or dare I say even mix, we are doomed. What is so in the world is that no one has his or her finger on the pulse of God, i.e., we all have a right to our opinion and existence. But no one's opinion or existence is more divine than the next. We must come to the realization that different is not defined in terms of good or bad, right or wrong, but simply meaning not the same. It seems that variety is the spice of life everywhere but with human beings.

What is it that causes different to be perceived as so scary? Is it in our DNA to be excluding of others and to back off from those who are different? The answer to that is **NO!** What is so is that we are drawn to those who have similar likes and dislikes because it's easier and feels less threatening. What I mean by this is that we are going to naturally seek out those who are interested and can do some of the same things we do. An easy example is that those who are good in sports or with computers are going to naturally move toward each other, respectively. It has nothing more to do than with common interests and goals. There are too many people to be involved with and we do not have the time or the inclination to find out about each and every person that we can relate to.

Therefore, we will find those we can identify with and it is not about different but ease and comfort. It is about character and how it relates to what is important to us. Even those who are sports minded would separate out those who are in a particular event. Football players do not have the time or desire to hang out with the swim team members. That does not mean that either football players or swimmers are better or should be considered dangerous, it is just another example of different. We find those who we have something in common with because it is easier for us to identify with, and we do not have time to explore all other variables. However, it does not mean that because we can't easily relate that difference connotes evil or dangerous.

We live in a world that is forever different. There is nowhere we can turn without seeing the diversity that is life. Whether we are going for a walk and experiencing the wonders of nature or sitting at an airport watching people on their way to somewhere else, we are struck by the contrast we see. In fact life and its wonders would seem pretty boring if we did not have differences to compare. and contrast.

If we accept the reality that everywhere we look the most natural thing to expect is that nothing is the same, then why do we have such a disdain for the differences in each other?

In the musical "South Pacific" there is a song that speaks to prejudice and in one of the lines of the song's chorus it states, "...that you have to be specially taught," i.e., prejudice is something that one has to learn, it is not something that you come into this life with. When toddlers are around other infants their senses will tell them that another toddler is a different gender, color, height, weight, etc. This however does not deter them from seeking out another child and playing with him or her. They do not see differences as bad and in fact pay very little attention to them. They base their desire to interact on more internal aspects of the other child. Do they like to play the same games, is there a proximity to the game or the other child, is there a chemistry for the other child that brings them together for play, is there an ability to share and compromise in how they use the toy in question, and is the other child able to play well with the other? These are the important issues at hand, not whether the skin color or religion is politically correct.

It is within this framework what I believe Dr. Martin Luther King meant when he said, "Judge a man not by the color of his skin, but by the content of his character." It should not originate with our "learned personality" of miss-beliefs where we assess whether we are to hang out with someone or not, but by how another human treats us and how we experience him/her. We have to "be carefully taught" to connect with our non-different friends, i.e., those who we are told come from the same backgrounds and do not pose any threat or embarrassment to the façades around us. What is the interesting part of all this is that there is no living being on earth that is not different than us in some way or another. The rub is that society tells us how far those differences can be pushed or allowed. For instance it is OK if you are Caucasian to be friends or date someone who has an awesome tan, but if someone with the exact same shade as your tan friend is Native American, Hispanic, or African American then this is probably not going to be considered a good thing. Why? Because we (whoever "we" is) say so.

By the time you are halfway through grade school everyone has been given his or her invisible rulebook of who is OK to associate with and who is TOO different to hang out with. At this point there is very little leeway for those who do not have the "right" status and credibility to be part of the accepted. Difference has taken on a societal definition of "bad" no longer to be considered just dissimilar or God forbid interesting or exciting.

What causes such a thing? Well, as stated in the above, people have a need to be around the safe and familiar. The more people feel like they are in an environment that they know and can predict, or are at least familiar with, the more safety or security they experience. Those of you who have raised or been around children know that they thrive and relax the more you can provide routine and consistency.

They feel safest when they know the lay of the land and who is in it. There is even a phenomenon known as stranger anxiety, which is when infants are more prone to outbursts when they are around unknown people rather than their primary caregivers. As an infant this makes a great deal of sense since they cannot protect themselves and need to feel that they are not in harm's way.

However, the rub comes in when we teach our elementary school children out of our own fears passed down from generation to generation that we need to carry on a learned stranger anxiety. Thus we are perpetuating an inner learned sense of being unsafe in the world. However, instead of taking responsibility for our own insecurities, we project onto others negative qualities that perpetuate a distancing from them gaining a false sense of security.

Now this goes way beyond the appropriate vigilance of watching out for danger in places where danger occurs. For instance, were you truly sitting in front of a lion and felt fear, this fear is valid and justified. The type of anxiety I am talking about is like sitting in an empty room and worrying that you will be attacked by a lion. This anxiety though conjured up from miss-beliefs, projections and learned panic, needs to be taken seriously. Therefore the best and only way to keep safe is to be hyper vigilant and distant from that which is different, while staying in the proximity of that which is familiar.

So with this as your mentality, you go through life constrained, closed off, fearful, hypervigilant, self-prophesying the negative, on guard, and leery. What a way to go through life, eh? **NOT!** It is like a child who cannot take care of itself and must always run from or hate that which is not familiar.

OK, so let's look at this. Gerald Jampolsky wrote that "the opposite of fear is love." Therefore, if you live in the fear that different is bad and to be watched out for, what does that do to your capacity to love? <u>It shrinks it</u>. If you live in fear then you must guard your heart and not just your body. If your heart is armored during your waking hours, how easy is it for you to take off that emotional armor and relate? <u>Hard!</u> I tell my patients that if you live in fear you cannot live in faith.

So now it gets real interesting in that as loving and religious as you thought you were, now you see you are walking around out of the bounds of real loving and of being in faith. Remember, love, faith, and spiritual beliefs come from the heart. Many teachings are of divine love that we are all children of the Universe/God. If that is so, how can you proclaim your faith and belief if you are blocking the very mechanism that generates this feeling? Answer: <u>you can't!</u>

For those who are less dogmatic and more spiritually inclined, this affects you in much the same way. We know that being in ones' truth and intentioning, a la the laws of attraction cannot be accessed if we are shut off. Only when we are in our witnessing perspective and expanded in our divine selves can we manifest that which we want. So clearly no matter how spiritual you believe yourself to be, if you are signed up to the mainstream belief that different is bad, guess what? You're clearly out of self and faith as well.

Spiritualists are those who know that we are all souls having a human experience, and if you are in fear of the many, what does that say about you? How can you be walking your walk if you are afraid and anxious of God's other children? And yes, there are those who are in this life who are to be feared because they are predators capable of causing damage. But most of the people you would define as different are not a threat to you, and deserve your respect and compassion for their soulful walk-not your judgment and distain.

So now we are talking about being out of touch or cut off from accessing your soul. If we are constricted and in fear, we are unable to connect with our higher selves where your witnessing, intentioning, and abundance are accessed. Also there are many religious and spiritual texts that say 'that as you believe it so is it done unto you.' Therefore, do you not see that by living in this projected perspective of negativity and constriction regarding difference you are not only cut off from others and what they have to offer, but your self as well? Thus living in a nowhere place that personifies the slogan, "life is a bitch and then you die" or the glass being half empty, or simply not getting most of what you want in life.

From this perspective you have not much more than a day-to-day existence. You are not able to taste the full flavor of the passionate fruits of life. So many young people I work with have trouble accessing their passion and feel depressed at what they perceive as the futility of life. Who would have thought that by owning the socialized sense of different being bad that you become one of the socialized walking wounded? No wonder anti-depressants are the most prescribed medication in America.

This issue of different being bad comes up more directly for me in my work with couples. So many of us look for someone who is in sync with us regarding common backgrounds, values, morals, goals, quality of life, and family. However, as John Grey has pointed out that as different genders we have a host of things we do not perceive or relate to the same. When you take that into consideration plus the fact that we are all different in the way we were raised and the emotional baggage we carry, if you don't attend to these differences, relate to them and accommodate them, your marriage will be in trouble. Hence, after five or ten plus years, this is what I see in my office: a marriage in crises.

It never ceases to amaze me that no matter how long people are together they forget to focus learning about each other so that they take into consideration the differences between them. From this perspective the love is blind thing kicks in and we overlook the warning flags and proceed as if "it will all work itself out." These famous last words keep me in business. People want to believe that this other person is like them and they don't want to recognize the differences. It always amazes me (and my patients) that in a few sessions I know the warning signs and where the land mines are in their relationship better than they who have been together for over a decade. Though this may seem magical, it is only observation.

Couples don't really observe each other; rather they are more in an expectant mode. They want what they want and can't understand why they are not getting it. And instead of putting their cards delicately, tactfully, and respectfully on the table, they act out their hurt feelings in many different ways. This occurs because our inner child wants to be given that which it did not get growing up and is not happy that their spouse is not getting it. Well, the reason spouses are not getting it is for two reasons, one they are not us and two they have their own agenda of what they are looking for from us. Therefore, both partners after many years of not getting what they need, and feeling unfulfilled just distance until one or both of them is looking to get out or hook up with someone else.

WIFE: *He just does not know how to treat me anymore. I feel like I am taken for granted and that there is no appreciation for what I do.*

DR. R.: *What is it you would like for him to be more aware of?*

WIFE: *He is extremely busy and I understand that he is preoccupied but there is no recognition of what I do for the family or how I look. I can put on a new dress and he has no idea that it is new.*

DR. R.: *What goes on for you as your wife relates her concerns?*

HUSBAND: *For the most part I think it's crap. I have always been attracted to my wife and I just can't imagine that this petty stuff is important. There is so much more to deal with in our lives than this.*

DR. R.: *What happens for you when your husband dismisses your concerns and says that there are many other things to worry about?*

WIFE: *I understand that we have some real life issues to handle and that he is stressed about them. However, I feel hopeless that there is a way for him to see what it means to me. I understand he loves me and it is nice to hear that he is attracted to me but it takes coming here to hear it.*

DR. R.: *What it like for you that your wife knows that there are pressing issues to deal with but that her connection to you is waning due to a lack of appreciation?*

HUSBAND: *I am sorry that she feels that way but after the time we have been together we both feel unappreciated.*

DR. R.: *How do you feel unappreciated?*

HUSBAND: *Well, I don't think she has a clue what it is like out there and how hard I work to make ends meet.*

DR. R.: *What do think of that?*

WIFE: *I know how hard he works but all I hear is how grateful or lucky I am that he does.*

DR. R.: *Ok, let's talk a little about the difference between men and woman a la John Grey's* <u>Men Are from Mars, Women Are from Venus</u>. *What you both are talking about are the different ways men and women look for appreciation. Traditionally, men need to feel like their hard work be seen and appreciated while women need to feel like they are appreciated for what they do and how they look. Though this may sound somewhat chauvinistic, Jung calls them archetypes. This basically means that from the beginning of time men need to feel honored for risking their lives out in the "jungle," while woman need to feel honored for attending to their domain. What do you both think about that?*

BOTH: *I can see that I am probably remiss in letting her know that I see her. I can also see that he does work very hard and I probably don't say that enough.*

DR. R.: *There is more to work on, but this would be a good start. Instead of waiting for the other to acknowledge you it would be good if you could both step up with letting the other know what you appreciate in the other.*

Another example of differences in couples is:

WIFE: *I feel very disrespected by my husband. Every time I go to him with something that is bothering me he tells me it is unimportant and then proceeds to tell me how to deal with it.*

DR. R.: *What do you think?*

HUSBAND: *I don't get it. She has these issues with her counter-part at work. It seems to be a no brainier. I handle things like this all the time and I know exactly how to handle it.*

WIFE: *You see how he believes he knows and I don't!*

HUSBAND: *If you don't want me to help why do you come to me?*

DR. R.: *This is very typical in relationships. Men are linear and problem solvers. They react from a place of fixing things. Women are processors and need to vent and get things out in the open and off their chests. Often woman come to men to discuss issues and what they want is to be heard and empathized with.*

WIFE: *Yes that is exactly what I want.*

HUSBAND: *But I am not doing anything.*

DR. R.: *Yes you are doing something but not like you are used to. Your wife first off wants to be respected for what is impor-tant or an issue for her. Telling her that what she is dealing with is a "no brainer" is diminishing what is important to her and judging it from your perspective. Additionally, em-pathy says you understand who she is and lets her know that you get her and see how she feels.*

HUSBAND: *See, I'm not doing anything.*

WIFE: *Do you see what I am dealing with?*

DR. R.: *It is not your decision on what is important to your wife, and she needs you as her partner to support her. This is done by listening and letting her know you get her. It is disrespectful to assume you have an answer for her and she doesn't. It implies you see her as inept and ineffectual.*

HUSBAND: *Is that how it makes you feel?*

WIFE: *Yes.*

HUSBAND: *Don't you know I think you are very bright and competent in your work?*

WIFE: *I know, but you take over the conversation and tell me what to do as if I am an idiot.*

HUSBAND: *I am just trying to help. I never meant to disrespect you.*

DR. R.: *What helps in these situations is to understand the different places you are coming from. If one of you goes to the other to relate something it would help if you first let the other know if you want help problem solving or someone to listen.*

TO EACH OTHER: *Yes that would help if I knew what you wanted.*

DR. R.: *It is important not to judge or run through our own intellect/computer what the other is saying or needing. We are different and we need to be respected for that and given what we need from our partner.*

I guess there are certainly more things to say about this, in fact probably a whole other book. However, in not being particularly prolific or research oriented, I have no need to do that. I am working at keeping all of this as simple and to the point as possible. I am not here to wow you with facts and details, but to get you thinking outside of the mental "software" box you live in. To see that difference is not as otherwise proclaimed, the poisonous apple to be avoided at all costs. Rather it is a wonderful, stimulating, and glorious spice of life's variations offering each of us growth and personal expansion. And since differences in every day life are unavoidable, wouldn't it make sense to enjoy and learn from it rather than hide out in fear?

One of the ironic aspects of this fear and insecurity is that it is derived from those whom we thought were divine and flawless guides put in our lives to teach and protect us. As it turns out these gods of our early universe were none other than the ever flawed, human creatures called parents. The rub lies in killing the myth that these humans were divine entities.

CHAPTER 9

KILLING THE MYTH

What myth you say? This is one of the deepest and most severe contributors to the miss-beliefs consistently sabotaging your personal actualization and empowerment. It is the inner child's inability to let go of the miss-belief that those who raised him thought to be divine gods (herein lies the myth) were actually human beings called Hank and Sara, i.e., parents. Subconsciously the sense of who we fully can be is on hold waiting to be blessed and given permission by these illusionary divine beings. Until that occurs, we are on hold waiting to go out into the world and "become our fully actualized self."

The learned personality, described earlier in this book, is built on compensating for who we believe we are "not" (for the purpose of this book: our miss-beliefs) attempting to be loved for who "they" (our primary caregivers) seem to want. In this way, we keep hoping to do whatever it is that we must have not done to be blessed by the divine. Only in this way will we feel a deep sense of permission to go beyond that which we have learned we are "not" and "can't." as we go about attempting to do it "right" for "them" thus we subconsciously hold our lives in ambiance waiting to thrive.

Due to this waiting, feelings are suppressed and behaviorally acting takes its place manifesting in a way that sabotages your social and/or vocational worlds. You may say this is nonsense or psychobabble, but it happens. And you know is occurs because it keeps happening to the tune of bopping yourself on the head wondering what it will take to have "this" acting out stop.

Another way you know you are a victim to this myth is how often do you find yourself surprised that one or both of your parents act or come across in a way that hurts and disappointments you? You have known these people all of your life, and yet you will get off the phone with them surprised at how they responded to you. What is it after all these years that still surprises you? This always startles my patients when I ask them this question. Because the logical, obvious answer is that nothing after all these many years should be surprising at all. And yet it is.

The answer is that when we call up our parents we are not calling the human beings we have known all our lives. We become the inner child calling the divine mother or father "hoping" to get a benevolent being on the other side of the line. And when we get the same ole same ole human who does not come across divinely, we are disappointed and depressed. Once I explain this, patients often have the epiphany as to what is going on. The inner child will want to fight me on this as if saying; I can get them to be the divine beings I want. All I have to do is figure out what it is

I am doing wrong that keeps them from offering me what it is I need that they surely want to offer me. As they say this, the adult will smile and get sad at the obvious lack of this being a probability. Once this kicks in, the discerning divine from human commences.

This provides the adult a chance to see what is real even when real "stinks." I also let them know that they were cheated to the extent they wanted to be honored and blessed. I add that if their parents could have offered what they needed, they would have done it years ago. Additionally, any expectation that their parents will show up in this way is folly, hence a myth. I usually emphasize this by redundantly saying, it will never, ever, ever, ever, ever happen. I do this not out of a need to be sadistic, but the inner child actually needs to hear it this way to truly take it in as every aspect of its being wants to believe this just ain't so. To truly take it in means that all the years of "waiting" and thinking that it was your fault was also a myth. This only created a miss-belief that you are inadequate and not worth being adored, which was a waste of your time and energy considering the source.

An example of this is:

CLIENT: *I keep trying to get my wife to listen to me and understand how hard it is for me to anticipate.*

DR. R.: *Aside from realizing that you are "trying" what gets in your way of anticipating?*

CLIENT: *Thanks for reminding me that I was trying. I want to talk to my wife and let her know that I feel like I am unable to anticipate or even think in those terms.*

DR. R.: *What gets in your way as you attempt to do so?*

CLIENT: *That's the worst part is that I don't even get that far.*

DR. R.: *How so? If I were standing by you as you even thought that there is a need to do something what would happen?*

CLIENT: *I would tell you that I see that something may need to be done and then I get distracted, lose my focus, or just say, oh well.*

DR. R.: *What would you guess is going on?*

CLIENT: *I don't know.*

DR. R.: *Guess even if it's not right.*

CLIENT: *As I start to check in I feel like I am just not able or adequate for the task.*

DR. R.: *Where is this familiar in your life?*

CLIENT: *Everywhere.*

DR. R.: *Pick a card.*

CLIENT: *Well you would probably like me to look at my parents.*

DR. R.: *If it fits.*

CLIENT: *My dad used to always watch over me when I would start a project. I would not get too far into it before he would step up and tell me where I was going wrong and what to do.*

DR. R.: *Okay, how did that feel?*

CLIENT: *Like crap. I always felt like I could not trust myself and that he would catch me at it.*

DR. R.: *Is it possible that every time you even begin to think about a project, you sabotage it because you still believe that you are not up for the task?*

CLIENT: *My head tells me that it's ridiculous, but my gut resonates with what you are saying. You think I am still expecting him to step up and make me feel inadequate.*

DR. R.: *I think the "little boy" inside is waiting for dad to say you can do it and until that happens you are staying low so you won't have to hear it. Unfortunately, what that does is sabotage your relationship with your wife because she knows and expects you to handle things, and partner with her.*

CLIENT: *So subconsciously, I am waiting to get him off my back and therefore making my wife crazy with my procrastination.*

DR. R.: *Yes.*

CLIENT: *Okay, so how do I get rid of this?*

DR. R.: *What is your father's first name?*

CLIENT: *George.*

DR. R.: *Your little boy is waiting for his divine father to show up and offer his blessings. He is holding your adulthood hostage thinking that to move without this blessing will just bring more criticism. So what do you imagine would happen if you hung around or did projects hoping for George to give you his stamp of approval?*

CLIENT: *Huh, George does not have a stamp of approval only a sledgehammer.*

DR. R.: *Right. So how long would you have to wait and how long do you put off your being able to anticipate and accomplish for George to bless you?*

CLIENT: *[with a sad laugh] Forever.*

DR. R.: *Right. This is our next step of the work, but you are seeing where we have to go with this.*

The important point is that as long as you keep subconsciously hoping that your human, flawed parents are the divine beings capable of unconditional, altruistic, completely healthy divine parental offerings, then you must believe that you are that unworthy, less than, not to be given to child. As long as you hold this myth of who they are not, expecting and waiting for what they can never give, nor ever had the capacity to give, then you must keep your self in the one down, less than, inadequate child position. Once you realize that they are not capable of giving you what you want and never were, you can let your self off that subconscious hook holding you back and move on with all you can be with regard to relationships and your career.

To be able to maintain this awareness and let go of the myth, I next invite my clients to remember who they are calling and to stay diligent on that. Thus when you call up your parent, remind yourself that you are calling Hank or Sara, not the divine beings you have been longing/waiting for. Because to the person, when I ask them if Hank or Sara could offer the blessing and sense of worth that they want, the answer is always a resounding NO. Once this is clear at a deeper subconscious level the feelings of grief, and anger can have the room they need to express due to the years of mythical hoping. And these feelings are not light or easy. It is no easy matter to grieve that you have been sabotaged and stagnant for most of your adult life. The important point is to fully grieve the loss of those adult years and opportunities gone by. In doing this both feelings of loss and anger will allow you to keep seeing the real picture and in essence make a pact with your self never to invest in this myth again.

The good news is that you can actualize the rest of your life from here on. Only from the place of being healthier and beginning to move on from the myth and stagnation can you have the perspective of how unhealthy the past subconscious behavior has been. I reinforce for those I work with that only from being more consciousness can you realize why and deal with these tough overdue feelings. Only from being healthier can you know this. Therefore, that you have to deal with these feelings means you are coming out the other side and able to truly move on for your life and for your self. The rewards of coming out on the other side and moving on for your self are what the next section is all about.

SECTION II

THE REWARDS OF GETTING THERE

This section of the book is the fun part. The first part is about the work of undoing the learned subconscious miss-beliefs that have plagued your life and caused you in some manner to be in your way of getting "there." This is the learned personality that shaped and molded you into the "lesser" person you did not particularly want in terms accomplishing your purpose in life.

In this second section, you get to relish in the prospect of the rewards of doing all that unlearning. It is the place where you get to not only own the rewards you have earned, but are now entitled to them (in most of psychology entitled is a very bad word; you never want to have someone think that of you and you certainly don't want your therapist to use that word to define you). It is akin to meeting and excelling beyond the defined goals of your job, and being entitled to the bonus that comes with it.

This is about the bonuses you have earned as you have processed the work; preferably with a competent psychotherapist (a well-meaning friend just won't do; sorry, it seemed necessary to say that). You finally get to throw out most of your subconscious trash (now I say most because number one you do not have to get it all to benefit from your work, and number two eradicating it all is just not realistic).

The things that will be discussed in this section have to do with diminishing the ego to the degree that you are letting go of the "learned personality" so that you are not shackled with miss-beliefs that sabotage your successes. Additionally, you get to indulge in the rewards of feeling freer than ever before, more fluid manifesting self, having as Deepak Chopra would say, a detached caring stance of being the witness, and empowered with your divine truth and proclaiming it. You will also be able to reclaim and embrace your deepest level of what I call your divine true essence of self.

Can you imagine stepping out of the ego, being more of the witness, feeling freer, knowing your truth and proclaiming it? It's possible. You will also find out how to sow the right seeds on your path, effectively learning your lessons and facilitating more growth and wisdom. You will be able to scan people's strengths and limitations without even meeting them, enhancing your own serendipity and empowerment. Most of all, you will be able to remember and embrace who you are at a deep and divine inner place of your core.

CHAPTER 10

REMEMBERING WHO YOU ARE

One of the great joys resulting from taking out the trash through learning our lessons is remembering who we are beneath the core psychological DNA learned from childhood. We are not our learned personality, and need to reclaim the true divine being that is underneath our ego defenses manifesting in how to "get along" or at the very least survive. These survival traits have been around so long, if not lifelong, that we think this is the reality of who we are. It is a joy and a reality shaker to come to the realization that we are so much more.

There is this essence of self which is at the depth of who we are. It is so remote and unfamiliar to us that we have almost forgotten it. We have metaphorically put it so far down a dark hall in our psyche that we are almost completely out of touch with it-our divine self. It is the core of our most treasured sense of self that owns our greatest sense of joy, sensitivity, passion, intuition, expression, energy, and personal gifts.

It is not that we don't have some of it at our disposal, but when we suppress our emotions we aren't given the luxury of just the "bad ones." It is not just the sad, hurt, betrayed, angry, sullen, depressed feelings that get put in the suppression container, but all of our emotions are dumped into it to some degree. Now when we go after our emotions, it is the tough ones that first show up since they were the ones that caused the lid on the container in the first place. As we reconcile these wounds, our more positive/helpful emotions start to come into the light and grow stronger. As this occurs, we become more whole and complete. One exercise around this has been detailed in the first section. It is the one where you visualize sitting in a dark hallway with a candle and invite your wounded inner child to come out and listen, which is very effective.

To remember who we are, is not to create something new, but reclaim our suppressed, essence of self. In the bible it says something like, to re-enter the Kingdom of Heaven, we must become like a child. This does not mean we are to become childish, but to be in that honest and spontaneous sense of self. If you have been around children, you know that before they get too heavily indoctrinated with socializations of do's and don'ts, they are very real. If they want to play, they do. If they are hungry they let you know. If they are sad, angry or happy they display that.

It is this perspective of being real that I believe is the attribute of "the inner child" that gets one into heaven. It is where one's quintessential self in all its truth and realness is apparent. It is this that we all must reclaim. The place in each and every one of us that is alive with realness and walking in one's truth. Only here do we behave as self and allow our essence to shine and be visible. It is here that Marianne Williamson's statement used by Nelson Mandela in his inaugural address emphasizes what I am talking about:

> Our deepest fear is not that we are inadequate. Our deepest fear is that we are powerful beyond measure. It is our light, not our darkness that most frightens us. We ask ourselves, who am I to be brilliant, gorgeous, talented, fabulous? Actually, who are you *not* to be? You are a child of God. Your playing small does not serve the world. There is nothing enlightened about shrinking so that other people won't feel insecure around you. We are all meant to shine, as children do. We were born to make manifest the glory of God that is within us. It's not just in some of us; it's in everyone. And as we let our own light shine, we unconsciously give other people permission to do the same. As we are liberated from our own fear, our presence automatically liberates others.

This, to me, is one of the most insightful, wise, profound, and life affirming statements existing. This embodies what I mean by reclaiming our essence. This is the ownership of our empowered self that allows you to enter the Kingdom of Heaven on Earth manifesting all that anyone could want or dream of in their deeper self. It is taking ownership of our true inner power and strength that we were taught to suppress because others could not handle us.

We are brought up to hide out and constrict ourselves so that others can "tolerate, allow, include, care for, and be with us," ensuring that we are not alone or rejected. Of course this is nonsense, but more prevalent in our upbringing than any of us would like to believe. It is this very lack of acceptance of our greatness that causes us to put that inner child in a dark room in our psyche where no one will point a finger or claim we are unacceptable. Therefore, we live in our own made up hell of fear, constriction, insecurity, low self-esteem, depression, resentment, disdain, victimization, negativity, etc.

All of this causes us to walk around the earth less than, and wondering why we feel so bad about ourselves or excluded. None of this has to be, and yet it is so prevalent that antidepressants are the number one selling prescription medication. What's Up With That? Well now you know! It is that we were programmed to believe that we should be afraid of our greatness, in essence our own true self. So, once again it is not that we have to create something new to become more; it is that we have to reclaim our inner, hidden greatness.

As we are able to access this inner divine greatness, we also reclaim the gifts that came with it. Most of these we are unfamiliar with, while the others we are out of practice with. Some of these gifts we use to a limited degree, but in reclaiming our selves, we can have even more access to them and begin to see them expand. We were born to make manifest the glory of God that is within us. To experience and bathe in the majesty of your gift and feel the confidence, joy, and esteem that comes along with personal greatness is the best. It is true joy, akin to what the mystics call bliss. We get to know what it is to have pride in our selves, which is void of ego and self- aggrandizement. This begets a sense of being humble because you recognize that this gift flows through you, but does not originate with you.

As this becomes clearer, you can see that your gift is a divine one and you are proud and pleased to be the conduit of it, cognizant that you are not the owner it. This is how I look at my gift of being a Transpersonal Psychologist. As I sit with my patients I am aware that I step out of what is called my self and make room for that which flows through me and accomplishing the work. I often chuckle at seeing that the insights that flow through me are ones I could use for my own growth. I sometimes hear myself commenting inside how wise a statement something was, and that I need to apply that to my own journey. Hence, this is why I rarely take credit for the good work that people see me doing. Mostly, I am grateful to be the vehicle of such work that has the ability to change people's reality no matter how long they have seen themselves and their life in a certain way.

This is one of the true gifts of taking out the trash and getting out of your way. In this moment we get to reclaim our inherent nature as my friend Dr. Rick Moss says. We get to not be something different and new, but remember the divine being we are. The being that has been too long shoved aside believing it is the worst of us rather than the most of us. We reclaim that which has been too long touted by those wounded gods of our upbringing as wrong, annoying, hurtful, too honest, too loud, too much. Instead we get to own its magnificence. We get to come back to ourselves and by doing this it "sets us free" to walk and experience everything and avoid nothing.

In this freedom, we now have the capacity to move around and expand our awareness, our joy and our sense of empowerment. It allows us to be in the passion and greatness of what we have come to schoolyard earth to do. When you can do this, it is the best of a work situation; you can't believe you are getting paid for doing something that comes without effort, feels so good, provides something good for others, and you don't resent getting up in the morning to go do. Is this bliss or what?

To walk in life this way, brings a glow to your being and lightness to your step. People around you will come up and ask what is it that is different about you? They clearly sense that something is up, but as they cannot read energy they will look for tangibles to explain the difference. They will inquire if you got a haircut or that those clothes or colors really work on you. They will not be able to fathom that you are in your essence, where the gift of who you are and what you bring to others is present and glowing. But the good news is that you will know the wonderment of walking in the exquisite light of your inner truth.

CHAPTER 11

THE POWER OF LIVING IN TRUTH

Another joyful reward of doing your work and taking out the trash is reclaiming and remembering who you are at a divine level. Thus being able to tap into and utilize your core truth. One cannot talk enough about this thing called truth. It is extremely important, but not because it is dictated by laws or society. It is because that living in truth will let you live to your fullest potential. The two quotes that embody this is Shakespeare's, 'To thine own self be true," and "The truth shall set you free" (John 8:32). It is the utmost in the definition of truth as it relates to who you are and your inner most sense of being able to successfully navigate your self and path.

The first step to reclaiming your truth is that if you don't know who you are, how can you check into self and find your truth? The reason it is a reward of taking out the trash is because you have dumped the miss-beliefs that have contaminated and clouded your sense of self. Hence it has dampened your ability to hear and feel the resonance of your truth ringing. You no longer have to react from these learned miss-beliefs and therefore have real access to your deeper self. As you have this access, you are able to go deeper into your very nature as described in the last chapter and resonate with what is "so" for you. As the truth rings, you are able to hear the ringing, know what you want, and what your exact next move is to get there.

How does this happen and how do you know if you're there? It happens because you are more available to your self and your inner sense of feeling, wants, passions, and desires, which all resonate from the heart. It is the learning to recognize or interpret the tugging of the resonance that is the key. This is the fascinating part of all this because truth cannot be put in your hands, it cannot be seen, it can not be shown to someone else, and it can not be picked up and held in your pocket when you need it. So what does this mean in terms of owning and recognizing it? Well, it means that though it cannot be produced for the eye to see, it can be felt at a level of certainty that is never misread or doubted.

To begin to own your truth like all other processes, you have to go through many trial and error episodes. Like anything else, this is a learning process of feeling and recognition. It starts with baby steps of reaching into your inner gut sense of things and see how it plays out. For instance, you have an inkling that you need to go left or right, a certain food is better for you today than another, you need to go and see somebody sooner than later, there is a place you need to be for no apparent reason, staying home is the right thing to do today, or you have a strong sense about something that is unexplainable.

If you listen to this "tugging" or "pull" and it turns out well or if you don't listen and have a sense of "darn, I should have listened to myself," both are examples of your barometer resonating your truth. This is the trial and error learning from your choices regarding your truth and the outcome that manifest from them. If you listened well, memorize the place that the feeling resonated from so you can recognize it when it happens again. And if you didn't listen, memorize the place anyways. You will always experience this in the same fashion. It is not a trick or a guessing game. The truth rings at the same pitch, and from the same place. All you have to do is pay attention, experience it, respect it, and act on it.

Now many of you may say, that sounds easy enough. But it isn't. The reason it is not easy is that the mind will want to ardently debate you out of such a non-linear perspective. It just makes no sense to the mind that something so intangible and nonsensical could possibly be correct. The mind deals in facts not feeling; it doesn't trust intangibles and is sure that something bad will happen to you if you abandon logic. It is attempting to protect you, while causing you to actually go astray from your true path. Not that the mind intends for this to happen, but it works in this way nonetheless.

This is why the process of owning your truth has to be a trial and error one because the mind will fight you tooth and nail to keep control, even though your desire to be in truth wants to succeed. So you have a tug of war going on inside between learning to memorize and trust the resonance of the truth, and the mind's attempts to talk you out of it. Eventually, you learn to say to the mind, stop it! Thus you learn to not give in to your mind screaming and turn over trust to your inner truth, which keeps showing up to be moving you towards your best interest. As you have more and more experiences, and realize that the truth knows its stuff, things keep turning out in your life for the better.

An example of this is:

CLIENT: *I have been thinking about owning my truth and how it goes. I think I have an example of this.*

DR. R.: *OK.*

CLIENT: *I was with my cousin and she said that she wanted me to read a philosophy book on something she believes in. I felt very strongly that I did not want to read this book. I know my cousin's philosophical beliefs and I know that it is not for me.*

DR. R.: *And what did you end up doing?*

CLIENT: *Well I like my cousin a lot and I know she has only the best intentions for me and though my sense was not to take the book, I did.*

DR. R.: *What was your mind saying at the time along with telling you about your cousin's intentions?*

CLIENT: *Well, that's just it. My mind went off telling me that it is just a book, it won't hurt me. I don't want to hurt my cousin's feelings, I am bigger than this, I can read something and not get side tracked, and why not.*

DR. R.: *Isn't it amazing how much logic and debate our minds/ ego can deluge us with all the reason in the world to go against our Truth.*

CLIENT: *No kidding. I was mindful of what was coming up and still it was hard.*

DR. R.: *Yes it is hard because all the logic makes sense.*

CLIENT: *Yes. There is little to argue with.*

DR. R.: *So what did you do?*

CLIENT: *I took the book home and realized I did not want to read it. I felt the resistance and the next day I took the book back and told my cousin it just did not work for me. It is as you said, trial and error learning.*

DR. R.: *Yes. This one was benign and did not cost you any- thing. This was an easy error that offered lessons without any* *pain. You got off lightly and got to see how it works. You went against your Truth and later realized that this was the wrong move for you. You got to see how the mind will debate against your/its own inner Truth, and yet goes against it. You also got to feel and remember how the Truth tugs at you. Remember this resonance, how it feels and where it pulls from. It is this and only this that you must listen to and follow as it never, ever lies.*

CLIENT: *You're right. It was an easy lesson and I will pay more attention to this.*

DR. R: *It is not to say that it won't happen again, but the more you are reinforced for listening to your Truth, the more you will learn to trust it.*

Once you have reasonably cleaned house with regard to your insecurities, there is a divine sense of your own self-awareness. It is in this place that one gets an deeper awareness of what makes you tick, what your passions are, and what is right for you. Some have called this the essence of self; some have called this being a righteous person. Most importantly, it has no deceptions, pollutions, hidden agendas, Machiavellian strings, or a need to destroy another person. It is why I say it is clean. Actually better than that, it is an accurate and true barometer of how you feel, what you want, what you don't want, and what you will and won't allow in your world. Additionally, you know when someone wants to cheat you, hurt you, lie to you, scam you, or betray you. On the other side, you also know when you are truly liked, included, cared for, cherished, and loved.

An example of this is:

CLIENT: *I am really noticing where I am listening or not to my Truth. Lately my brother wanted me to sit down and listen to him about his concerns for me and my shifting beliefs. I told him I would listen but only as much as he wasn't judging or demeaning. He started with his usual lecture on what I wasn't doing. I felt my Truth barometer resonating loudly and interrupted him and said I would not be interested in continuing.*

DR. R.: *How did that feel?*

CLIENT: *Great. For one of the first times in my life I knew what I felt, I knew what was OK and not for me, and it was actually easy to step up and say enough.*

DR. R.: *Why do you think it was so easy?*

CLIENT: *I know I asked myself the same thing. Somehow I felt stronger and more clear. The sense of enough just seemed to bubble right up to the surface. I also said it without anger, or going ballistic, or disrespecting him. Pretty cool eh?*

DR. R.: *No, very cool. This is what we have been working toward. An inner sense of empowerment in which you know what you know.*

CLIENT: *I am not sure what you mean?*

DR. R.: *For me, the reason you set your boundary and told your brother "enough" was because at your core you knew what was best for you.*

CLIENT: *You're right.*

DR. R.: *When you listen to your truth you have a clear cut sense of what is OK for you to be a part of and not. From this core place of knowing you react easily and strongly without having to pummel the other person. In your clarity and firmness you let the other person know it is enough.*

CLIENT: *Yes, that is exactly how it felt.*

DR. R: *When we are in our Truth which always Knows, we react with clarity, assertiveness, and ease. When someone is not serving your best interest your Truth does not have to get a second opinion.*

Now, I know you may be thinking, who is this guy and what has he been smoking? No one thing can do all that and be dead on accurate a hundred percent of the time. Really? Isn't it true that when you have all the viruses out of the way and good programming that your computer will always get the right answer, is it not true that if programmed right your GPS will get you to the right location all of the time, is it not true that if you input the figures correctly your calculator will always come up with the right answer? If so, then why is this so hard?

If you can take in that we are all polluted with emotional hardware viruses (subconscious miss-beliefs) causing us to come up with the wrong answer for our life, which sabotage getting you to where you want to go, or getting it right-what is so hard to believe about this? The hard part is getting rid of the hardware virus. There is nothing easy about this, and it takes effort and the right kind of technician to help. And the worst part of it is that unlike a computer where you take out the motherboard and reprogram, a human being is not so easily or quickly rewired. It takes a relatively long time due to variables like the subconscious and emotions, which do not let us go any faster than our hearts can stand it or feel safe.

I know that many of you do not want to buy this notion for one second, while some will take it as a challenge to see how fast they can rewire. What I say to all of you is, go to it! And when it does not work, just remember that your heart like everyone else's heart will not go any faster than it can feel safe handling the dark, scary, threatening side of itself, which is where the work of rewiring miss-beliefs occurs. Hardware is hardware, and substantive change is substantive change. It is the most important, courageous work you will ever do, and it will take time. So instead of bitching about how long it will take, get to it.

This is the ultimate in taking out the personal trash and being in truth. It is the inside, deep work that puts you in touch with you. The rewards of which are living in an inner truth which will <u>never</u> lead you astray, whether it's accessing your passions, what your body needs to eat, which road to drive down, where to park your car, what profession to pursue, or how you feel about someone and they about you. It is the quintessential barometer of your exactness.

Needless to say, to have this tool cleaned off and available to you is the real deal. It is the most important contributor to your walking your path/life in the most appropriate self-enhancing way, facilitating your being in your higher self. Your truth barometer gets sharper and sharper the more miss-beliefs you clean out, and cannot be accessed if you have not healed/taken out most of the trash. Whatever intuitive, gut instinct you know you have, there is more to be had. This "more" will allow you to walk a freer path unencumbered by dogma and expectation than you could have ever imagined or previously embraced.

CHAPTER 12

FREEDOM

The most rewarding or self evident gain for taking out the trash is to walk in the world without an attachment to outcomes or opinion. Most of us cannot even imagine this let alone do it. It is what is being vulnerable and empowered all at the same time. It is where you can be in your feelings and your intellect and not be a target. There is an old Zen saying, "they shoot arrows but do not find a target." This means that the world you walk in is still antagonistic and though people throw out sarcastic zingers or are downright mean, it does not have to affect you in the slightest.

When we are clear in our center as to who we are, then we know and accept our strengths and our shortcomings. In this fashion, we are focused in our true nature of self and own what is so for us. Therefore, if someone is hostile to us, being open to our feelings makes it clear we are being attacked and we can then take immediate action to confront or deflect the attacker.

An example of this is when I was invited to speak at a conference and the C.E.O. of the company came up to chat and introduce himself. He walked up and in typical male fashion he took a sarcastic shot at me. I looked at him and said, "Ouch." He looked at the ground as if he had stepped on my foot and said "What?" I said, "Did you mean to put me down by that statement?" He looked at me and with a chagrined look on his face became speechless and walked away. Now there are many retorts I could have used here, but the important point is that my sonar is up and aware when someone is attacking me, which is never okay. No one is going to get by me as long as I am true to myself. Thus, one is very cognizant of what is happening around him/her when you walk in your truth, i.e., vulnerable/open to how you feel, while empowered.

It is not that we need to get over on anyone; it is just that they do not have the right to get over on us. Thus, whatever your response may be, it attends to the situation at hand and is therefore a win because you take care of you. It is strictly a defensive move to protect, not an offensive one designed to hurt. Most martial artists will tell you that fighting is the last resort. They will employ whatever is necessary to assuage their antagonist, but when all else fails, they are prepared to do what they must to not be in jeopardy.

I believe in options. Therefore if we are caught up in an emotional maelstrom, then we are incapable of realizing possibilities. We are then only able to employ one or two survival techniques hoping not to die. When we are in this mode we are on a survival plane that does not allow for expansion, openness, or being able to choose the best way to handle something. Being open to your truth gives you a detached quality; a knowing that will guide you to the best way to defend yourself against those who would try to diminish you, or take your power.

An example of this is:

CLIENT: *I was recently at a family event and due to the aware-ness of my self I've gained working with you, I realized that my uncle is a mean son of a gun.*

DR. R.: *What happened?*

CLIENT: *Well I am amazed that I have been getting ambushed by this guy for years.*

DR. R.: *How so?*

CLIENT: *As we have worked on the issue of defining sarcasm, I am clear that is how he relates to people and especially to me. I was witnessing him as you have said, shooting arrows at me. It is clear to me that he has wounded me on more than one occasion.*

DR. R.: *It is interesting hindsight to see how we have given cer-tain people the right to hurt us.*

CLIENT: *Isn't that the truth. He always tells me how special I am to him and that out of all the nephews I am his favorite. But I now see the cost I have been paying for that and I don't like it.*

DR. R.: *What has the cost been and what did you do about it?*

CLIENT: *The cost has been that he says how special I am and then he zings me with an arrow. I am here to tell you it hurts.*

DR. R.: *Yes it does. It is probably unconscious on his part, but it is like you get a big hug from him and wonder how that knife got in your back.*

CLIENT: *No kidding. So after he pulled one of his zingers, I said to him your word, ouch. He looked at me as if I was nuts. He said, what happened? I said that statement hurt. He did what you said sarcastic people do, he told me I was too sensitive. I told him I was not and that as much as I loved him that was not OK. He grumbled and walked off. Later he still came up and gave me a hug, but no zingers.*

DR. R.: *Yes, it is surprising how when we firmly set our boundaries people back off.*

CLIENT: *Yea, it's great.*

DR. R.: *What is important to see is how unconsciously you have been enabling and giving permission to your uncle to shoot his sarcastic arrows at you. And as you are more conscious of your self and therefore listening to your Truth you are taking better care of your self. Your uncle no longer has permission to attack you. From this position of empowerment, you have the option to do what is necessary and thus you are free from attack and allowing put downs.*

In this place of serenity and composure, overwhelming you is not possible as you are in the zone of the Tao: a zone that is always flowing and never on the hunt. One walks as a merchant I knew in New York. He was out for his lunch break and walked through a busy part of New York as if he was strolling in a meadow. He was not naïve or stupid, he was centered in his body and though keenly aware of his surroundings, had no fear. I reveled in the wonderment of his stride and demeanor. I realized that it could be done, if you can live in the freedom of your own awakening.

This awakening is the manifestation of being without ego. It is being in life without an agenda that feels the need to be more than others or show up better than others. In essence, you are not validating yourself by how others perceive you or admire you. It is the walk of someone truly content in their own being, which is not about anyone else's definition of who you are. Therefore, there is no sense of being scrutinized. There is no sense of having to live up to some expectation, what you should look like, or how you should behave. You are an entity unto yourself without catering to a predisposition of what others want.

Now most of us have no idea how to do this. It may seem like a noble idea, or something you would read on a fortune cookie. Most people conduct themselves and their business as if the world holds a report card over them and is waiting to waylay them with a failing grade. Again, Eleanor Roosevelt said, No one has control over us we do not give permission to. From this accepted, considered normal state of being, most people subconsciously through learned conditioning, and/

or socialization give this permission to others on a daily basis. From this perspective, it is almost inconceivable that we could or even would want to reclaim this control or terminate giving permission for others to control us. We continually play the game and stay in "the matrix" of a pre-described environment that we think brings us joy. We were brought up that this is the "way," and most would feel that they were employing sabotage to act in any other manner.

Walking in the freedom of the divine self is the ultimate joy. Only as you step out of the game and truly understand the absurdity of the superficiality and one-upmanship out there can you understand what I am taking about. To embrace life in this way does not cause sabotage, instability, craziness, isolation, or failure as we were brought up socialized to believe. It is the path of strength, empowerment, and joy. As you know I love movie quotes and this one is from *War Games*. The quote is, 'the only way to win is not to play.' I use this all the time with my clients. It is so poignant with regard to day-to-day life. Most of us look to outsmart the game instead of just choosing not to play it. Now this does not mean don't work, or forgo the proper education. What it does mean is don't submit to their rules and their playing field.

There are certain things we may choose to do their way to get the job or the degree, but we don't have to lose sight of who we are and why we are there. In other words, pursue what you want and get the training to get there, but don't buy into the way they define it or you. Remember, you are the only one who knows your inner truth and who you are.

I have two Masters degrees and a Ph.D. I did this because there was a certain place I wanted to get to and that was the course. However, I was always somewhat outside the box and never let "them" define me or who I was becoming professionally. The human race needs to put everyone in a box because it feels safer, hence the chapter in this book on difference not being bad. In this way, my professors wanted me in that proverbial box for their own peace of mind. I never gave that to them. I did the work and learned my craft, but always from a vantage point of knowing who I was and where I was going. It was frustrating for some as well as for me because my professors had a sense of my difference. However, I also found professors who enjoyed and supported my difference, as they had some of that as well. Nonetheless, I successfully completed my studies and practice in a way that moves patients to their higher selves.

The forefathers set down in the Declaration of Independence that each of us has the right to pursue life, liberty and happiness. They did not dictate exactly what that was, nor did they state that there was only one way to do it. They employed the notion that each of us form our own definition of self and truth manifest his/her own sense what life, liberty, and the pursuit of happiness is for ourselves. And that each of us does this as long as our actions and choices do not infringe on another persons' right to pursue their understandings of this. They clearly understood and put down that it is not about one-upmanship or competition, but the encouragement of all freeborn people (as they described free born, of course, we know they left out races other than Caucasian and women) to be their highest selves. This is the height of spirituality and wisdom. I believe they got at a deep level the discernment of non-competitive individual enhancement, while separating out the normal competitiveness of business. This is freedom, and in this country up to and including now, many of us have lost the understanding of what this truly means.

To undo the work of the "trash" brings us home to the core freedoms of life, liberty and the pursuit of happiness. These are rights that we all own which have been inadvertently relinquished. As the subconscious miss-beliefs are worked through and mitigated, the freedom to pursue ones gifts, passions, and purpose on this earth truly as granted by the Declaration of Independence and the Universe/God. And all of this gives rise to something so completely unexpected as to boggle the brain: the ability to scan and read people's minds.

CHAPTER 13

ABILITY TO READ MINDS

Once you have moved into the witness state and have the perspective of watching the play, your ego takes a back seat and is not involved with assessing the goings on around you. As you get more familiar with this way of seeing and come from your unencumbered truth, you begin to realize that you know things about people in a whole new way. You begin to notice that you are accessing who someone is without any tangible data. This sounds completely beyond belief and almost ridiculous as if out of Star Wars or something, and yet completely doable. As in the old adage, you can only love others as you love yourself, which means owning the perspective from inside to out (described in an earlier chapter).

As you evaluate yourself and free up the ego embracing the witness, hence becoming inside oriented, you can then assess and evaluate other people through an inner sonar projected out like an energy field, much like a sonar dish on your rooftop. The difference is that instead of just receiving information, you are scanning outward first then receiving data back.. Therefore, you realize that you know things about someone without talking to him or her, or getting input from anyone else as to who they are, what they are thinking, what they are withholding, and if they are coming off truthful with regard to your relationship. It is not your tangible senses that you are assessing people with, but the intangible third eye and the energetic field, which we all have access to as we do our work and get out of our own way.

This is not mindreading in the sense of knowing their every thought, but sensing exactly who they are and how honest they are coming across in the moment as if they were hooked up to a lie detector test and you were reading an assessment of their strengths and weaknesses., In essence, you are reading the very emanations of someone's field as to who they are.

FRIEND: *So you believe that you have the ability to scan someone you have never met and know things about them?*

DR. R: *I think everyone has this ability if they do the inner work of getting out of their way. This takes being more aware and doing the hard work to really know more about yourself as well as being vulnerable to your limitations. From this perspective, one can then send out the sonar field that can gain information on just about anyone.*

FRIEND: *What would cause you to <u>not</u> be able to do this?*

DR. R: *Well there are a couple of situations that come to mind. One is that the person you are wanting to scan has done their work and are not walking around with their issues so apparent. This individual would be harder to read. A second possibility would be someone who triggers my buttons causing me to shut down by feeling threatened or insecure. This person would alert me to my work but it would not help you to get the information you would want.*

FRIEND: *OK, see that guy walking across the room downstairs with the blue suit on?*

DR. R: *Yes.*

FRIEND: *Tell me what you are picking up about him.*

DR. R: *Well he carries a strong sense of anger and being arrogant. He feels to me like he is less than honest and would not be someone who would validate you or give you reinforcement. He is not a team player though he comes across like he is with charm and personality. As deadly as he is in business he is very bright. He seems like he would be in your face challenging you on your ideas, while giving you a superficial sense of a job well done. He is not someone I would trust and he does not seem to me like he would have in depth relationships, though he acts as if he is liked by many. He reminds me of that statement in the movie, The Bronx, "Would you rather be loved or feared?" This guy wants to invoke fear. I would also not play* *poker with him, He never wants to lose and he can bluff like a son of a gun.*

FRIEND: *(There was a prolonged silence that actually caused me to look over at my friend. His mouth was on the floor and his eyes were so big they were about to fall out of his head). That is exactly who he is and I should know as he is my boss. How the hell did you do that? That is not possible. My boss prides himself on the fact that he carries who he is so close to the vest that no one can know him until he wants them to. He actually says that with arrogance and pride.*

DR. R: *It is not a trick, but a result of doing the work of cleaning your own house and then looking clearly into the house of others.*

To those who wear blinders and live within the box, (or like in the movie *The Matrix*), this will seem like some sort of bizarre magic or B.S. To those of us who live outside the box, or matrix, it is common sense "seeing." This so-called magic is available to all us who do the work I have described in both my books. We are all beings of light with gifts beyond our tangible sense of things. This gift comes with the work, but you do need someone to mentor you along until you understand more clearly how to fine tune your energetic scanner and how to interpret what you are picking up. This, like most processes, is a trial and error one with a definite learning curve. It is about trial and error because our logic wants to be in control and have a tangible say over this radar. It does not want to believe it can work and certainly not outside the purview of linear thinking.

Therefore, as we venture into this new world, we will project rational assumptions into the mix rather than let the sonar give us the data. As we are mentored through this process we are taught to discern the difference between the two. As we use trial and error, and succeed more than fail (and learn from our errors), we harness and hone this skill. But once you are on your way, there is very little that can fool you with regard to truth or manipulation. The reason for this is the truth as I am talking about rings and resonates in a manner that is dead on and unmistakable.

Think about it. How cool would this be in your life, and what would you give to be able to use this gift? My guess is, whatever it takes. Well it takes having the courage to do your shadow work deep in the places that you don't like to talk about or feel. But as you do this most important work you begin to step out of your script and your patterned role and take the witness position. A position embracing the empowered place of being and learning without the drama of life. As this occurs you are able to step into what seems like the twilight zone of scanning and knowing who someone is. We can call it reading minds because that is what others will think you are doing. The reality is that you are getting sonar/energy faxes to your center and interpreting it.

CHAPTER 14

WITNESSING

This is an interesting aspect of dumping our garbage, as it is something we all can do and is the healthiest and most spiritual perspective in how to lead/live your life. However, as you saw the word spiritual, how many of you still roll your eyes or sigh? Yes witnessing is a term often used in the Far East and is associated with many of the Eastern philosophical ideologies. But that does not make it any less relevant to being, living in the west, and utilizing its perspective to enhance life.

To describe this phenomenon I will use analogies and metaphors to help give examples that will help make this clearer. However, the ones who have rolled their eyes may be wondering how they could have gotten so suckered in by what they have read to end up dealing with such an unreal Californian ridiculousness as witnessing. I assure you this is not the case, so bear with me.

Dr. Bill Little, as I pointed out in the first chapter, used the two-bird analogy to offer an explanation of witnessing. As he said, we are a culmination of two birds sitting in a tree. Most of our day-to-day lives are like the first bird that flies down to the ground and is caught up in the every day objective of finding worms to eat and dealing with the competitive other birds. We are caught up in the goings on of work, family, world and local events, while keeping our selves sane. We really don't get the time to contemplate our lives, as we are doing all we can to stay afloat amidst the many things we need to take care of, or that need our attention. We are caught up in the rat race believing that this is the deal and we just have to do the best we can.

The deeper aspect of getting off the survival level or at least the day-to-day routine is to seek personal growing and expanding through learning lessons involved with the ego. This perspective, which is like the second bird who sits perched above, is available for observing and assessing. This is hard for two reasons: first, it is hard being detached enough, which allows us to be removed from the process. Second, Western socialization is opposed to introspection, and strongly encourages people to distract themselves with as many things possible or be judged as lazy. Hence the encouragement is to not think of yourself as anything more than the first bird; superficially caught up in the drama of life.

The second bird is obviously the witness. It is from this perspective that you are not caught up with the goings on of the ego and can have the distance necessary to observe, reflect, and shift. It is only from the world not being in your face, so to speak that you can do this. The next quote is one of my favorites and gives another analogy through metaphor for the witness. It is one of Shakespeare's from *As You Like It*:

All the world's a stage,
And all the men and women merely players:
They have their exits and their entrances;
And one man in his time plays many parts,
His acts being seven ages (II.vii. 139-143).

Eric Berne wrote a book in the seventies called <u>Games People Play</u>. In it he speaks about the scripts people play out. The stage and the players that Shakespeare is talking about is the first bird as is Dr. Berne's scripts and games. It is the day-to-day roles that we play through life, acted out in the scripts we are given from childhood that make our lives seemingly rich and successful. It is this indoctrinated script of western living that socializes us to aspire to external success and validation, which by the way is also referred to as the American Dream. Not that there is anything wrong with this, but it is not everything (I will elaborate on this later).

So, if the first bird is analogous to Shakespeare's on stage players, then who is the second bird? Like the second bird who sits high above the daily action and is for the most part out of sight, the witness analogous to Shakespeare metaphor is the person sitting in the audience who is watching the play. This person is detached and not caught up in the ongoing play and has the availability to assess and learn from what is taking place. It is from this vantage point that all of us can observe our interactions within our own play, but not be a part of the drama. It is from this perspective we are able to learn from the roles being acted out in front of us. We can see our own ego at work and how it may or may not serve us. It is not that we are uninvolved in the script on stage, but that involvement is detached and only there to show us where we are insecure and in need of growth. It is in this way that we see how far we still have to go to be in our real, divine, and truest self.

As I mentioned earlier, on my radio show, *Heart and Soul with Dr. Bill Little,* we call this "souls having a human experience." Therefore, we are both the birds. We are the human, a la the first bird or the player who is walking through life/ the play doing the best he/she can with the cards or script given us. And let's be clear, we are given these cards or the script from early childhood by parents, community, culture, socialization, religions, mentors, and teachers. Often people will say to me that there lives were laid out for them and they just had to plug in the holes. Others will say they were told by those around them that doing such and such was the path to fulfillment and happiness. I tell them that this is what gave definition to them as human doings not human beings.

The soul is the second bird witnessing from a detached place, observing and learning. We come in with our soul and we leave with only our soul. Hopefully, we have more of our lessons learned during our life so that we won't have to return to schoolyard earth, or at the very least can move up the ladder of evolution for the next life experience.

Thus, the witness is a higher consciousness where we are able to detach, evaluate, and learn. The trick is how do we do this? Ah, as Shakespeare would say, therein lies the rub. Though there are some too wounded to ever recognize, honor, or admit being damaged, most of us have some observing ego that wants to see and learn. This observing ego is desirous of growing and invites epiphanies. This is normal and most people have epiphanies intermittently and what are also known as wake up calls. Every so often, one will pop up, and if we are open to it, personal learning will occur. If not, we put out head back in the sand and stumble along until the next eye-opening tap on the shoulder.

Oops, I got somewhat off track. How do we do this witnessing thing? We have to do the work described in my last book, The Road To Me, along with the trashing of one's miss-beliefs described earlier. As we do this, every one of us is able to step out of our way and not be so caught up in our ego as the first bird is and the players are. We really get that we are not our script and that pecking the ground competing against the other birds is not the best use of our life. The old cliché I like relating to this is, work smart not hard.

As this registers, a metamorphosis takes place where we begin to sit back and own our detached perspective. As we sit in this over time, we begin to see that we are more than we thought and our self-identity is not caught up in every drama, and are not on notice with every challenge. With this, we are not drawn into the drama of life and others what I call "stuff." We can discern the difference of a behavior and personal identity. Also, we are less available to being challenged and react only as one who is watching the play, assessing the roles; detached and untargeted. Once we are seated in the audience of our own play, we are less reactive, more pensive and thoughtful. Our perspective is one of compassion and understanding for the other players who still believe that the stage is all there is, and the script is all they are.

Thus as we embrace the witness we come into focus retrieving more feedback on our behavior and interactions not biased by our ego; hence as we dismantle the data, we grow and learn from a deep substantive place in our being. It is through this devotional journey of inward evaluation, thus freeing your self from the data of the "learned personality" do we begin the journey to remember who we truly are. It is not that we create a whole new person, but we reclaim the whole person already within us. It is not recreating the mousetrap of self, but allowing the phoenix to rise from below, free of most of the misperceived trappings of the learned/virtual self. Hence, this is the divine path to our true self and what I believe is the prelude to enlightenment, hence being there. It is where the trash of the polluted self is dumped freeing the inner true nature of self to emerge and take ownership as an empowered being who walks the earth with confidence and truth. It is the soul working out its karma through walking this learning ground called human experience.

The next part of being in the detached witness state means having a keener sense of your higher self, inner truth, or some may call it, the soul. This voice of higher self/inner truth/soul speaks to us, though it may sound like your own voice with a more developed sense of wisdom. However you want to tag it, it speaks to us continually from our higher self of knowing. For who else could it be that speaks to you from that inner voice of prudence, insight, direction, and wisdom? The purpose of this can be debated;

even the existence of what I am saying can be questioned. However, if you are in sync with this line of thinking then you know what I am saying is true.

This is not to be confused with experience alone. That's different. This perspective is our inner voice of reason and wisdom, but it is clearly not originating from our typical intellectual base of knowledge. We get messages, or directions, that seem to be given to us as if we had a consultant hidden away inside. This consultant offers us information and answers that get our attention due to its higher state of awareness in the messages than we typically assign to our own intelligence. It just doesn't seem to originate from our selves, and yet it does come through us. A movie I would refer you to that exemplifies this inner consultant is *Always*. In this movie the main protagonist dies and is brought up to the next step to be told that it is his turn to guide someone in his profession as he was once guided. It is made clear that the insights we get and the gift we may have for doing a certain profession or talent is due to the mentoring of one who has passed on. They are giving us the guidance we need to do our work well.

It is my intention that we surrender the ego by unlearning our miss-beliefs and become one with the Universal antennae. From this Universal airwave we let go, retrieve information and download the data. These Universal airwaves seem not just to impart basic information but wisdom. Think about it. You have probably experienced this at least once in your life without needing to delve deeper into the occurrence. The situation just seems to kick in as you let go of wanting something.

Another example would be trying over long periods of time to answer a difficult question and then as you give up or let go, the thing or answer just shows up, not a memory but the answer. This happens because you surrender your intellect and allow the Universal antennae to do its work and download the information. The debate could be whether this is a message from our collected life times accumulated in our soul experience, or from a channel that is there to guide us on a higher level. I tend to believe we get messages from both sources, but this is a debate I will not embark on now. Suffice it to say that your soul shines while your human experience has more of an ease to it. As this happens, not only does your life shine brighter but you begin to see that you are becoming the creator of your own reality.

CHAPTER 15

CREATING YOUR OWN REALITY

There's a Buddhist quote that says something like, what you believe is what you will experience, and in quantum physics it is every action has an equal and opposite reaction. My friend and radio co-host Dr. Bill Little, who is also a physicist and minister, told me something about what physicists had to attend to when they were first dabbling in particle theory. He said that as physicists were working on their experiments they were taken back by the reoccurring fact that as they expected particles to go a certain direction, they did. This self-fulfilling prophecy stunned them as they realized that they were having influence on something that should have been definite and out of their control. It seems to be a global truth that as we intention anything we have influence on how it comes about and the outcome in specific. Now this could easily blow your minds as it did the physicists I am talking about. Not only can the future be manipulated, but directed toward where you want it to go and in a way which will benefit your life.

Wait - so what I am saying is that we are the creators of our lives and where we want it to go? Yep, that is what I am saying. So how do we do it and how cool is that? Some of you will think Bull S..t and want your money back for the book.

As a friend of mine, Dr. Rick Moss, creator of Precognitive Reprogramming says, if you want to see what you want, look at what you have. Hmmmm, so if you can grasp this idea you understand that we not only live in a Universe that wants us to have abundance, but we are the culprits who are in our own way of allowing the Universe to fulfill our intentions.

Let's start with the first part of this, that we can create our own reality and that the Universe is waiting to give us what we want. I have noted that many orientations subscribe to this. It is not new, just not all together believed in. It is not believed because our linear Western society cannot deal with this notion. We do not want to buy into the fact that we have serious influence over how our lives go other than the all too typical notion of hard work and struggle, coupled with a bit of luck. We have trouble owning that we can create a reality in which we are receiving what we want for the sole reason that we have an intrinsic worth with the Universe. And yet it was Marianne Williamson's words made famous by Nelson Mandela in his inaugural address that states that "our biggest fear is our greatness not our limitations."

It is most difficult for us to embrace our ability to intention and be great. We do not want to believe that we could be powerful in this respect and impact reality. Yet, so many references are being brought to our attention through the media attesting to this very fact. The problem is that everyone wants it to be easy and simple, and when it is not they throw up their hands in disgust feeling suckered into believing such a ridiculous notion. We want to believe, but we want the fairytale version of manifesting. Once learned it is easy but getting there by dumping the unconscious trash is anything but simple.

The second part is where the not-so-simple comes in. This is where we must undo the complex levels of learned miss-beliefs that subconsciously run our lives. The reward for this is we can impact and create our reality. The rub is that we do not just wish for a Ferrari and it shows up in our driveway. We have to follow the intention with action. An example would be when I want to increase my psychotherapy practice I first thank the Universe for sending me more people. I act as if it has already happened and I stand in gratitude. The next thing I do is back up that intention with action. Remember the quantum physics law that each action brings an equal and opposite reaction. So I will go out and do a talk or a class to enhance my commitment to the Universe that I am serious about more. The interesting thing that often occurs is that referrals almost never come from the talk, not the organization, not the people who attend, not anyone who heard about the talk. The referrals come from somewhere completely unrelated to where I put my energy.

What I have surmised is that the action that is being reacted to is that I have put intention and attention to getting more referrals and they come. It makes me chuckle because there is nothing linear about it. The referrals come in the time frame I expended the energy, but not from the place where I expended it. Now there is someone who is reading this thinking if intention is all that is necessary because that in and of itself is an action to be reacted to by the Universe, why do you have to do more? This is a great question because the answer should be you don't. I will own that I too am a western-raised linear guy who is not perfect at this. Therefore, I hedge my bet by doing an additional action as well. However, I have more recently gotten to the place where half the time now I will intention and thank the Universe for sending me more referrals and nothing more. And you know, around the time frame I do that, referrals come.

Another example I will give you is when a friend of mine and I go out to lunch, I will intention parking spots opening up. My friend is a devout non-believer. I will tell him where a spot will open up or that a spot will be coming up soon. We both chuckle at the fact that most of the time it happens. He will offer some "reasonable" explanation as to how this occurs. This is not magic, it is not luck, it is not co-incidence, it is not hocus pocus, it is as you believe so shall the Universe meet you. And as the Universe meets you it is on board with your desires and intentions to be successful in your endeavors.

CHAPTER 16

SUCCESS

Another surprise and reward in the grab bag of dumping the subconscious trash is success. The more we get out of our own way, the more we can have all cylinders firing on whatever task we go after. Not only do we have our hearts and minds on board, but also every level of what is talked about with regard to law of attraction, intentioning, and the energy of the Universe. How can this be, you ask? Again, remember that physics law dictates that with every action there is an equal and opposite reaction. As you step up from the many complex levels tangibly and intangibly with regard to who you are, the Universe reacts in kind.

For instance, if I asked you to break a board with your bare hand, you would look at me like I was crazy. And if you attempted to break a board with your hand, it would be your hand that would break. If you train with a martial arts expert, he/she will teach you to bring not only your physiology to the action, but your concentration, intention, energy, breathing, and the Universal chi energy that is the world. Therefore, you would be harnessing every aspect of force available to you in the Universe to succeed at your task, which seemed impossible to you before. Thus, your reality has changed as to what you can do and what you believe can be done. How is this possible? It is because there is more to our existence then you can almost imagine, and yet your awareness expands as you become more aware of it.

An example of this:

CLIENT: *You have mentioned that as you heal aspects of your self you expand and become more successful. What do mean?*

DR. R: *There is an old saying that goes something like this: Luck favors the prepared mind. Well it is not just luck that brings success. Successful people always talk about luck as there is always some of it that comes their way as they are making their successes. The ability to have a prepared mind is the trick. It not only means the tangible issues like doing your homework, knowing your product, your audience, and the competition, but it is so much more. It is the mental clarity of knowing what you want, knowing you can do it, knowing you can deliver, knowing you can be all you can be, having the vision to create, having the ability to lead others, being able to gauge that and reorient when necessary without being a control freak, and therefore having the wherewithal to expand yourself and not get caught up in petty ego battles that win the skirmish and lose the war.*

CLIENT: *Well if one could do that then how could one not be successful?*

DR. R: *Yes that is the deal. What that means is getting out of your way of being caught in an ego that is small, constricted, narrow, fearful, insecure, petty, acting out immature hurts and angers, and isolating. These are really all one in the same coming from a hurt inner child that is hiding out and lashing out to survive.*

CLIENT: *No kidding.*

DR. R: *No, no kidding. It is the work we have been engaged in and are pursuing. It is doable and possible as long as you hang in there and keep having the courage to seek your inner demons.*

So, when I say that as you do the inner work of self, more of what you believe and imagine expands as your perimeters of self do. Things you have read about or heard in a lecture now begin to become real and possible, instead of just theoretical. This applies to whatever you set your intention on whether it is martial arts or your vocation. As you get your self prepared to take on such a task, you direct your attention toward being on purpose; this means you attend to your task in a manner that is focused and more direct than ever before.

So many times, we believe we are doing all we can to get things done, but it is not true. Think of the times you thought you brought all of yourself to a task and then found for some reason cranking it up a notch or two. A minute before you would have thought that giving more was unlikely or impossible, and yet there you are a few minutes later utilizing more energy and drive than you would have thought possible.

How many times have you been in a working out, exercise class, dancing, running, bicycling, or any strenuous situation where you were sure you were done in. You were sure you had nothing left and nothing or no one could make you go another step. And then out of the blue some one you like or admire, or some outside stimulus showed up and beckoned you to go that extra bit. And you did. How could this have happened? Where did this extra surge of energy, spark, enthusiasm, or drive come from?

It came from the place that is your essence that is not connected to your mind/brain/logic/head that tells you that you are done. It comes from a place of knowing and gusto that is in and of itself. And somehow in that moment you tapped it. You tapped it because you got out of your head, your pain, you pessimism, and your negative sense of self and just allowed it. This is where the drive and power to be successful comes from.

As the subconscious trash has been diminished, your negative inner voice does not have center stage. You find that getting out of your way is becoming more and more natural. As time passes on and you believe that this drive and power to create, have vision and pursue dreams will not go away it gets more familiar. As it gets to be familiar you begin in a good way to take it for granted and expect to work at this level. You are out of your way in a familiar manner and bring more of you to what you are doing.

The analogy would be if you had an obstruction in your kitchen faucet, and as you turn on the water you get a trickle but not the full stream expected. No matter what you do, you will not be able to get the water to run better without more work. What has to be done is to get rid of the clog. Once this is done, the force and flow of the water is automatic. You are not surprised when this occurs, because you have done the work to unclog the faucet. You go back to expecting a normal flow of water when you turn on the faucet. So too is it with all the rewards I am talking about.

Unfortunately, most of us are not used to being out of our way and therefore, normal is being less. Once you begin to work from a place of being more, it will get familiar and then become normal. Until that time, you will wonder and analyze how this could be happening. Once you are familiar with you on full flow, it will become your new normal, and you will be grateful the clog has been removed and the full Tao of you is back.

Suddenly, success is not the scary, tedious, overwhelming thought of what ifs and second-guessing. It is not fraught with the familiar doubt and self-recriminations our ego typically employs because of those miss-beliefs listed above. It is a delightful embarking on a challenge that invites you to come dance. The "it" is an exciting adventure that has your utmost attention which is ready to embrace life. This is where we are completely in the moment with our intention and on purpose for the favorable outcome we expect. We are free to own our joy and desire, which facilitate and creates our walking in our empowerment.

CHAPTER 17

COMPASSION & HUMILITY

Another reward offered by dumping your subconscious trash is you are given an ability to walk the world with compassion and humility. Now before you warriors go off and throw my book away, listen for a second. What I mean by compassion is an outlook towards your fellow man/woman as he/she goes about their life, internalizing the offerings of life's lessons. As you realize that we are all souls having a human experience and this is not a competition, we learn compassion for each person's struggle. We are aware what it took for us to get where we are and have a compassionate perspective for others who are on their own courageous journey. Additionally, as we are grateful to have gotten further along our own spiritual path with the realization of the gifts that come with it, hence we are humbled by the experience. We can be proud of what we have accomplished as we walk with our heads metaphorically bowed. And as we let go of our egos, compassion and humility are two of the attributes we are rewarded with.

Humility is similar to owning compassion; in fact I tell people they are cousins to becoming our higher selves. Additionally, most men run for cover with this one along with compassion as it sounds like the first step to giving up your manhood. This occurs because we are brought up in a Western society that demands that men give up any feeling state for the facade of toughness and being continually unaffected.

The truly humble are those evolved people who have come to understand the wisdom that the more they do their work the more they realize that what "works" through them is to own it in gratitude rather than insecure boasting. What I mean by this is as Deepak Chopra has been quoted, we all have gifts we bring into this world to enhance it. These gifts are just that, gifts. What do you do when you get a gift? You say thank you. Most of us don't go around and boast of the gift, rather we own it with gratitude. Thus we own that this gift runs through us and from within us from a source that is not us. Though this gift is ours we did nothing really to create it. We may have gone to school or learned from a mentor how to hone it, but the origin of the gift is not us.

When one steps out of ego, a la insecurity and centers more in his/her truth, we begin to acknowledge the gifts we were given to walk this earth with. We utilize and enhance the gift and give it to the world, but with the understanding that we are using what we were given. This understanding is humility. It is not giving up the gift, it is not disrespecting the gift, it is not diminishing that you have the gift, and it is not being a wuss. It is honoring where the gift comes from and being proud how you are using it.

Now, as I finished the above paragraphs, I can imagine there are the jungle fighting machos and business warriors who are not considering this a perk of any kind. They cannot imagine that this is a plus, but rather a vulnerability or weakness that will get you figuratively killed in the competitive world of the corporate fighter. Well, I am here to tell you it just ain't so.

As we incrementally let go of our ego, we settle into that zone of the Zen proverb that states, *"They shoot arrows but find no target."* The more you are out there in an empowered place of strength, which we will talk about later, no one can really get to you. Therefore, if no one can get to you, you begin to relax and sit back in a place of peace. In this place there is no fear, vigilance, concern, only an amazing sense of invincibility.

Well, think about that – imagine having no real concern that any one can get to you in a devastating manner. That you can walk the earth empowered not being a target for anyone. From this place of safety and ease, compassion and humility for the others who are still unconsciously targets walking around seems obvious. Not only it is obvious, but easy. There is no effort wasted on how to guard up or strategize. You are using all your energy to stay truly you, humble and compassionate but not at risk. This is a place that I will speak about more in another part of this book, but it is where peace resonates and fear no longer exists.

It is the ego, fueled by the subconscious miss-beliefs that needs to puff up its shoulders, be competitive, and posture. It lives in the land that is mistrusting, unsafe, fearful, undeserving, guarded, anxious, vigilant, lacking in confidence, and generally concerned about success and acceptance. In this state one can only watch one's back and take the down and dirty road to win. The sad thing is that too many people live this way. There is no empowerment here, only a desperate compunction to control that which is not controllable.

When you are in the state of knowing, not trapped in the trash of subconscious miss-beliefs jerking you around, you are as I said earlier, free. This freedom allows you to own yourself in a way that is not susceptible to others' reactions or attacks. You have your X-ray vision going for you and you see the attack coming before they shoot. But even so, if they do shoot they find no target. As I wrote in my first book, The Road To Me, I love movie quotes and clips to illustrate my point. For those of you who saw *The Matrix*, Nemo just puts his hand out and stops the momentum of the bullets that were fired at him. In this same way, we see the verbal attack being fired, but it does not find a target because we do not turn our reality or validation over to the attacker.

Now of course, I am not saying that everyone who does this will get to the same level, but pretty darn close. If you continue with integrity to dump the subconscious trash, you will find yourself traveling down the wormhole toward self-actualization accompanied by an enlightened outlook on life.

Suffice it to say as we walk in our own world confident in our safety from verbal attacks, there is no fear. Without fear, we relax into a peaceful state of ease and expansion. In this state, we own the perspective of the witness, as we have compassion for other souls doing their dance on stage and hoping they learn their lessons. Also as stated earlier, due to mitigating our ego, we are humble about the gift we were given; what we know and what we have achieved. We have no stake in what happens and honor the Universe's plan for all, while we walk in a state of grace. This provides us with a wonderful foundation in the world and allows us to continue our journey toward being more. Again more comes from the consciousness and the wisdom we gain from learning our lessons.

CHAPTER 18

EMPOWERMENT

The culmination and greatest reward for taking out the trash of the unconscious miss-beliefs is to emanate empowerment. To be empowered is about taking on and owning ones strengths and limitations so that you are completely aware of who you are and who you are not, hence completely "there" with your self. This creates an internal solidity that offers each person that achieves it protection that is impermeable while maintaining complete vulnerability. For the purpose of this book, I will define vulnerability as being completely open and true to what your very nature is. Thus it is imperative that you know who you are and who you are not. Only when you are clear on what makes up the definitive you can you avoid being a target to anyone's attack.

Most people don't live in a gangland environment and therefore are not going to have to worry about physical threats. Most of us just deal with verbal assaults; sometimes on a daily basis. Verbal assaults are projected from someone's insecure ego that is lashing out to gain some personal power or edge over us. Only when you are insecure in your own right will the attacker have any leverage and be able to trigger your button due to insecurities that are raw and/or denied. As Eleanor Roosevelt said, "no one can make you feel inferior without your consent." Therefore, to thine own self be true takes on a clearer meaning. Hence, as you are definitively clear on who you are and are not, you will not be blindsided by an attacker hoping to get the drop on you.

It does not mean that you don't have insecurities, but they are not open to anyone's attack. So, if someone knows one of your insecurities and attempts to poke it, you see the attack coming. As you know this is one of your difficult aspects of self, you do not need to act out from it and can therefore react by confronting the attacker as to why they needed to take a shot a you. Most people will be blindsided by this response, as they don't ever expect anyone to be so empowered as to return the assault (however, your assault is completely appropriate though not taken to hurt or attack, but to defend and protect). The response you will get from most attackers will either be a physical or verbal withdrawal or back peddling. Additionally, the assailant will now be very cognizant that you are not someone they should mess with.

Once I had to go to court for a client of mine. We were all asked to the judges' chambers. As I was introduced to the opposing attorney who knew I was a psychologist he greeted me with "Nice to meet you Mr. Richman." Now he knew I was Dr. Richman but he wanted to keep a one-upped position or he was testing to see if I would allow this. My response to him was, "Excuse me that's Dr. Richman." He made an apologetic response and he never called me up on the stand, accepting my written statement as enough. My fantasy about this is that he saw I was centered and not easily intimidated. Hence he did not want to attack me on the stand, which would only hurt his case not help it.

A second example was with the CEO of a company I had just finished a consultation with. He came up to me after the presentation and made some sarcastic remark. I waited a second and politely said, "Ouch." He looked down at my feet as if he had just stepped on one. He asked me why I had said ouch. I replied, "Did you mean to put me down by that last statement?" He looked at me and the people around and walked away speechless. Now, this man was a client and obviously if I had wanted to be asked back I could have retorted with something else or not said anything at all. However, I did not care if I was asked back and wanted him to see his behavior. Whether he got it or not it was clear to him and others that I was not a target for anyone's put downs. Sarcasm is veiled hostility camouflaged as humor. If the target calls the person on it the two most common responses from the source of the sarcasm are either "you are too sensitive" or "I was just kidding."

My third and last example was when I was at a party with someone I was dating at the time. A friend of hers that I had not met came over to us and took a verbal shot at me. I looked at her and said "Ouch." She looked somewhat taken aback and said, "What?" I said, "Did you mean to put me down by what you just said?" She huffed, turned and walked away. My date turned to me and told me that she does that all the time, but had never seen anyone diffuse her that quickly. I replied that I do not let anyone put me down for their own shortcomings.

The knowing of self and taking care of your self is one of the many rewards of being in touch with your feelings. This is so contrary to what we in Western society and certainly men all over the world are taught. We are focused on strategy, linear responses, powerpoint presentations, and logic. To be aware of our feelings as a vehicle of empowerment certainly goes against the grain. But let's play with this concept for a moment.

If I were to shoot you, what would let you know you were shot? Your first response would be from your physiology and neuronal system, which would relay messages to your brain. From the feedback of that relay, you would then decide the best course of action. If an individual stays in his/her head and away from their heart, how would they know when someone attacked them? We can only know we are attacked if some feedback loop lets us know we are hurt, offended, triggered, antagonized, or angered. Once we feel what is going on, then we have the option to decide how we are going to handle it.

Believe me when I say that I have worked with many men who have no clue that they are being slighted or attacked. An example of this comes from a continuing education class I took recently. The speaker was one of those "guy guys," as I call them, who needed to focus in on someone and make them the blunt end of their sarcasm. The speaker was relentless at poking fun at the coordinator of the course, who in my mind suffered ongoing laughter at his expense. I walked up to the coordinator and asked what had he done to upset the speaker who made him the target of so much abuse. The coordinator looked at me and was startled. He said, "What are you talking about?" I said the ongoing sarcasm that is being leveled at your expense. He continued to look at me like I was speaking another language. He obviously was so used to the speaker's way of relating and did not even know when he was being poked at.

I knew what sarcasm looked like, but I decided to check in with a couple of guys at my table. I asked if they thought the speaker was taking shots at the coordinator. They both looked at me and nodded. It was amazing to me that the coordinator was so out of touch with his feelings, which is unfortunately not so abnormal for men, that he had no idea when he was being verbally assaulted. It is not uncommon for the men I work with to see sarcasm as a normal aspect of communication. Once I explain how it looks and the object of using it, most men get it (if you want to know more about this phenomenon you can go to my book, The Road To Me and look in the chapter on Defining Masculinity).

So this is the long way around to say that if you are out of touch that something hurts or affects you, how can you protect yourself? Only if you know you are being shot at can you respond. In the example above, the coordinator did not respond because he did not register a hit, let alone being shot at. Sadly, in not being able to register a hit, he kept allowing and enabling the speaker to hit him continuously. We must be able to know what is going on around us and certainly if we are being verbally shot at. This registering originates from the feelings, never from the mind. Once we are able to register danger, then the mind can make a decision on how to handle it.

The people who work with me often cannot tell me what they are feeling or reacting to. I tell them that I will play a game with them by guessing what is going on in them, and they are to let me know how close I get. Almost always they say that my interpretation is dead on. I then let them know that this is not magic, but by putting myself in their shoes and going deep into my feeling sonar, I can connect with what is in them. Though this understandably surprises them, they get what I am talking about. As they learn to interpret their own feelings, their sense of what is going on in and around them and what to do about it becomes activated. Thus, they begin to get what being empowered really means.

Again, the empowered stance is not used to win or get over on anyone, but rather to not let anyone attack or abuse you. In my early days of martial arts training it was repeated many times that this is not an offensive art but a defensive one. Shaolin monks are trained this way, i.e., they walk in humility, but are never defenseless. This is empowerment. It is walking from a perspective of being there in your truest aspect of self; with compassion and humility engaging with minimal ego, while not letting anyone subdue you.

CHAPTER 19

LEARNING OUR LESSONS

This next part is one that is an ideology that comes with spirituality, philosophy, metaphysics, and transpersonal psychology. It is a belief by those of us who believe in reincarnation that we are here in this lifetime to learn our lessons. Actually, not just this life but some that have tentacles back into other lives. However, those of you who don't believe in reincarnation may want to tag along, as you probably don't have an opposition to growing, learning, and becoming more. And, all those who never want to grow, mature, actualize, become more conscious, or want any benefit what so ever for your self, you may move onto the next chapter.

It is very difficult to learn ones' lessons if the ego is always rationalizing, denying, distracting, undermining, blaming, victimizing, acting out or ignoring input. When we have not done our work, much of this is what happens out in the world, as people do not what to have to deal with self. This is where the term, "get over it" got its origins. Only people who need others to ignore them, so they themselves do not have to "get real" are followers of the "get over it" regime. These are also the people who yell from the rooftops how stupid it is to go to psychotherapy, while also being contrary about it. Those of you who have or are doing their work of taking out the trash, you will find that you have a heightened awareness as to when the lessons show up. Hence, being able to take a closer look at what is that is supposed to be learned. Not only will you want to learn as quickly as possible to enhance yourself, but you are more open to the learning, get on it quicker, and do not find the lessons humongous.

Good deal, eh? Absolutely. As you are more available and present to prioritize learning, you find that the Universe hits you less often as well as softer.

We are incrementally relieved of the "stuff" of life, and can put our attention/intention toward more substantive life goals. This allows us to go far beyond what most think is possible. Each of us can excel to heights that we only could dream about or think was available to other more fortunate people.

But thinking about it, how often have you heard on your favorite talk show an acclaimed person saying that what they have done can be accomplished by anyone. They say that their achievements are available to all who have courage and invest the time to go the distance and learn their lessons. You know you have heard it more than once, but rationalized that you did not have the "special" something that clearly these famous people have. Rubbish! This is just your subconscious miss-belief jerking your chain, and sabotaging you from what you need to learn.

It is rumored that Deepak Chopra wakes up every morning challenging the Universe to bring it on! Whether he does this or not, when we have dumped most of the subconscious trash, we are open if not inviting the Universe to give us challenges that bring us to our highest self. We invite this because we are excited to learn more of our lessons so that we will unshackle our selves from fear and sluggishness. We are passionate and open armed, expanding to meet the day and be more. This is the end of a long journey where one finds oneself being truly "there."

CONCLUSION

BEING "THERE"

What does being "there" mean to any of us going through life? Some would say that life does not need to be so complicated. You just figure out what you are good at or want to be good at, work really hard at it, find a relationship if you want companionship or a family, find some friends to play with, have a hobby or interest, and "that's the deal." So many do not want to make it any more complicated than that.

What most fail to realize is how do we access our passion, which dictates what we are good at and who we truly love for the right reasons? If we cannot access this than the many tensions and difficulties which flare up due to behavioral acting out get in the way of our making healthy choices. Most do not want to recognize that the patterns popping up are unnecessary to their lives, and don't have to be tolerated. Most people don't believe that life can be lived on a higher plane than just mere survival or emotional suppression inviting dis-ease, drama, or that old familiar feeling of "it's just who I am." We can choose to live in a "tolerant" environment or seek a higher and deeper existence that offers self-actualization, health, and true joy. Or as the mystics say, bliss.

As long as we are stubborn, cowardly, in denial, rationalizing, blaming, assuming, judging and anxious, security driven, etc., we will be less likely to be on purpose or have the ability to truly step onto our path. As we continue with our Western heritage of only looking inches beyond our nose and only at goals that are self-serving to our ego, we live a lesser, constricted life. These choices bring us to the superficial; non-depth functioning that is all too familiar for far too many.

What is interesting is that many of us start out envisioning a grand purpose. We call it youth. Many young people start out with dreams of who they would like to be and what they would like to accomplish. As the road of life unravels, so many are told, "this is your lot in life." That the dreams you have/had are what we all start out with and that as we get older we realize that most of us don't get there. That it is in your best interest to write them off, get real and live with what life presents to you. Now some of that is true, in that we don't usually get all of what we wish for. We are confronted with life issues promoting our learning and growing. However, though this is true, what if we had shortcuts that spoke to the learning and realized that the goal of this learning is to be able to access our passion and have what we intention, how would that sound? Would you step up to that? Would you prioritize that? Would you shift your sense that things could be different and possible? My guess is, you would.

There is a saying in psychology that miserable people love miserable company. If most people buy into the premise that you can have more but not too much more, then they will teach, mentor, advance this notion to others. If I am not allowed to have most of what I want and I believe that, then I will teach it to you so I don't feel like I short-circuited myself. One of the ways this is propagated is in blue-collar communities or union towns, and is evidenced in the movie, *Rudy*. In the story, there are situations in which young adults want more for themselves than the factory lifestyle of their fathers. The fathers put down their sons' dreams of wanting to go to college and go beyond their family work tradition. It's hard for some or many of these parents to encourage their kids to go forward as they worry that their kids will be defeated like they were. They worry that such a lifestyle is for the well to do, which is not them. This sense of more is too scary and fraught with identity problems considered "reality;" not to be questioned or pushed. The concern is that if more folks were to make it, this would say to those who did not attempt it that it <u>is</u> possible. Psychologically, this would cause depression or at least some emotional distress for those who bought into the societal norm.

There are many who in this same vein of miserable people put down the validity of personal growth including psychotherapy. They tout it as only for losers and wimps who need to get with it and step up. They don't want friends or family to engage in this process as deep down they are scared of doing their inner work. Most of those who scream the loudest about how ridiculous personal growth work is are the very people who need it the most and are the most intimidated by it. This work is the road to being all you can be.

Most people want you to believe that who and what you are is it, and you shouldn't try to go beyond your self as you will only be defeated and put down. These naysayers will keep spouting the party line that it is silly, stupid, a waste of money, waste of time, only for the whiny and needy, not for the strong, a upper middle class joke, only for those without a life or friends, etc. Because if you were to engage in your growth and clean house of your subconscious miss-beliefs and go beyond your self (fully being there in your empowerment), then "they" would have to deal with being wrong. "They" would have to own that they are choosing to stay less, to stay stuck, to be constricted, to be dis-empowered, and to take ownership of the fact that they gave up on all they could be.

Unfortunately, our Western mentality is one of invalidating the veracity of this work. Our insurance companies show a lack of support for the mental health field vs. the support they give the medical field as anti-personal growth help. Certainly, the culture is clearly negative on mental health and introspective pursuits causing sabotaging behavior. We would much rather deal with shame, blame, punishment, divorce, and substance abuse than healing the underlying causes blocking personal empowerment. What would a society be like if we actually encouraged and provided appropriate insurance coverage with competent professionals facilitating a society of fulfilled, centered, conscious, actualized and happier people? Oh my God, what a nightmare--NOT.

How many of us really think in terms of having a distinct purpose that is clearly defined and pursued? To walk life with a purpose that entails personal and vocational depth, rather than just monetary goals or vocational advancement. To embrace mindfulness, which includes not only how we want to live life, but also how we want to participate in it. Mindfulness is the key word as it takes in all of what this book is about. To pursue being conscious much of the time with a purpose that guides us to be in our true selves in every moment - Being there. Therefore, to be on purpose and "there" is the single most important thing we can do in life.

To do this, we must work at it. Now I have been told by many of my colleagues, "don't say that." When you say that people have to do their inner, deeper work on their emotions and past wounds, it just makes them run for cover. If you want to sell this book you cannot say that to people. Once you say it, everyone will turn their collected backs on this concept/you, and go buy another book that offers the promise that they will "be healed" upon reading and completing said book. I guess I am just that naïve to believe more in the book reading public; that they are not that superficial, and they know that anything worth doing is worth doing well. I can't believe that the book buying public is so gullible that they would be duped into such unbelievable nonsense. And you know what my colleagues keep telling me-believe it!

Sorry, I got off topic. If you want to be in good physical shape, you work at it. And you work on it for the rest of your life because if you stop working out you quickly get out of shape. Well, so too with being more of self. You begin by working at it with a trainer and then you keep the routine going on your own. As you heal the wounds created by subconscious miss-beliefs, you become more whole, more "there." This begets you stepping out of learned tapes that have been running all your life. As you step out of the way of self, you step back from the other "birds" on the ground, you step into a deeper more removed perspective of the audience, and you walk from a place of empowerment. This place of "there" offers with it magical gifts that all human being willing to take the risk and put forth the effort can count on. These gifts have been laid out in the second section of this book and they are real and true. This is not some type of hype that is out of reach for the general public. It is there for every human being who is willing to "go for it." Friends often ask me, who is the target audience of your book? My response is always the same: anyone who breathes and wants more.

www.ingramcontent.com/pod-product-compliance
Lightning Source LLC
Chambersburg PA
CBHW070645290526
45790CB00001B/191